Advance Praise for
*the secret is YOU*

"Pure Romance is a story about the power of a dream and the will to break down the barriers standing in the way of that dream. Chris tells the inspirational story of how a business that started in a basement turned into a global phenomenon. But maybe more importantly, he clearly reveals that the same principles that were born in that basement, the bedrock of his company's success, still positively impact his company, employees, and customers today. Those principles can help anyone bring their dreams to life."

—**Rob Lynch**, CEO
Papa John's

"Finally, a book that shows you how to embrace getting outside of your comfort zone and how coaching, passion, dedication, and hard work are the foundation for accelerated sustained growth."

—**Bob Sumerel**, Founder
Bob Sumerel Tire & Service

"No business leader today packs more wisdom, energy, and inspiration per page than Chris Cicchinelli. At last, his unapologetic passion for helping people find their own personal greatness is captured in writing. This book will leave you on fire. Chris's energy is contagious—you'll love his voice, his story, and most of all, his ideas. You'll never look at yourself or your business quite the same way. I've already benefited from the ideas in this book in my own work. So will you."

—**Sarah Klein**, High Performance Business Coach and CEO
Sarah Klein Consulting

"Chris Cicchinelli is blessed with the rare combination of both high IQ and street smarts. He's a charismatic, passionate, and extremely creative businessman as well as a marketing genius. I am continually inspired by who he is. Chris's book gives us all an incredible opportunity to get to personally know him—and anyone who reads it will be richer for it."

—**Britney Ruby Miller**, CEO
Jeff Ruby Culinary Entertainment

"Chris Cicchinelli has built a unique business that is knocking the lights out. He took the risks and now is reaping the rewards, as his business is growing exponentially. In the process of building his business, he has also assembled a great team. Their momentum through the pandemic has been amazing. America needs more Chris Cicchinellis."

—**John F. Barrett**, Chairman, President, and CEO
Western & Southern Financial Group

# the
# secret
# is
# YOU

How I Empowered 250,000 Women to Find
Their Passion and Change Their Lives

## CHRIS CICCHINELLI

Post Hill
PRESS

**Post Hill Press**
New York • Nashville
posthillpress.com

Published in the United States of America
1 2 3 4 5 6 7 8 9 10

*To my mother Patty Brisben,*
*who made all of this possible.*

*And to my wife Jessica*
*and our children LC, Max, and Macie,*
*who make it all matter.*

# Contents

# If You're Reading This, It Means We Survived 2020

I have been kicking around the idea of writing a book for at least five years, and I'm pleased to have finally finished it—because it turns out that this is the perfect time to release a volume embracing my business philosophy.

Why now? Because we're just starting to crawl out from under a global pandemic that, as I write this, has claimed hundreds of thousands of lives and tossed everyone and everything into chaos. Restaurants, hotels, retailers, companies...all of them have had to ride out a year-long storm that continues to pose significant challenges even as you read these words. Many haven't made it. No one has emerged completely unscathed.

My company, Pure Romance, was as impacted as everyone else's when it all hit the fan in March 2020. Think about it: the core of the business is selling products at tasteful home-based parties. My job is managing the constant training and support of a remote workforce of thousands of women. Suddenly, with the COVID-19 crisis, people could no longer gather in groups, and for many weeks were not even permitted to leave their own homes.

And yet, we at Pure Romance somehow managed to successfully pivot and actually *increase* our business. Did this require a certain amount of luck? No question. But to a significant degree, we humans make our own luck—and when disaster came knocking, we were prepared.

It's true what they say: what doesn't kill you makes you stronger. We emerged stronger than ever before, in a way that would never have been possible had the situation with the virus never materialized.

No, we didn't exactly have a pandemic plan in place. What we had was a CEO (me) who understood going in that 15 percent of my life, or my year, is always going to result in something unanticipated. Here's the deal: when coronavirus showed up at our doorstep, I was thinking, "Hey, come on in. We've been expecting you."

So, while too many companies focus only on "growth, growth, growth, growth, growth," I'm always imagining growth minus 15 percent to account for any unforeseen issues. I find that most people and companies aren't prepared when that unexpected bill comes due.

Think about it this way. You have a washing machine. You know that at some point, it's going to break down. You don't sit back and think, "Gosh, now what do I do? I can't wash clothes anymore. I have to ponder this for a while." No. If you want to keep washing clothes, you need to have a plan in place for when the appliance stops working. You call a dependable repair professional, you figure out how to fix it yourself, or you toss your stuff in the car and go to a public laundromat. Or you buy a new machine. What you don't do is sit there paralyzed and twiddling your thumbs.

That's why they say luck is preparation meeting opportunity. When the virus temporarily rendered Pure Romance's longtime business model obsolete, we were ready to move into virtual parties without really missing a beat.

This was hardly an accident. In my world, at our company, there is zero chance for us to get lazy. I'm always suspicious whenever anyone maintains they should feel comfortable at work. Nope. Being uncomfortable is part of the gig if you want to succeed. It is, in fact, all about getting comfortable with being uncomfortable. When you're uncomfortable, you're ready for anything—including a once-every-century pandemic.

Everyone today wants instant gratification, guarantees, ease of use in this fast-food society of ours. It's all part of our entitlement culture. People crave immediacy. They want drive-thru diplomas. They want it *right now*, not even an hour from now. But that isn't the way to carve out a business niche.

I find that people spend far too much time worrying about the outcome, how much they're going to earn, how much their business will bill annually. But if you want to succeed, you have to understand the process that will achieve that for you and make it come to life.

Those who read this book will come away understanding that while change is inevitable, they must learn to flourish with each step they put into their business life and career.

Why should you listen to me? Well, for starters, I've helped Pure Romance grow from a $1 million company—partnering with founder Patty Brisben (who happens to be my mother)—to one valued at more than $350 million. Some 250,000 women have been empowered over the years to find their passion as independent consultants at our company. We have expanded not only across this country into all fifty states (as well as Puerto Rico), but also internationally, including into Canada, Australia, and New Zealand.

Understanding that our consultants who sell products in the field are the backbone of the business, until the pandemic I devoted more than two hundred days a year to traveling the world, speaking to the literally thousands of women who have made our extraordinary growth possible.

Some of these women, following a proven path, have thrived beyond their wildest dreams. I've heard stories of families in dire financial straits who utilized Pure Romance as a means of climbing out of debt and starting down the road to prosperity. I've also heard that it took their family's economic crisis for many of these women to learn about their assets, and that too often it was the men in their lives who were the keepers of all financial info. These women knew they had to step in and help their family make a plan for the future.

Also, consider this: at the beginning of my career, our company wasn't recruiting the graduates of Miami University, Yale, and Harvard Business School with summa cum laude honors. I had a team of people who were aggressive, who were hustlers, who wanted to grind it out all the time and get stuff done. I think over time I came to understand, just like leadership coach and trainer Marshall Goldsmith, that what got you *here* won't get you *there*.

If I have my choice, I prefer someone who's scrappy to a prodigy. I want people who will get in there and dig and not count on their intellectual gifts to help them persevere.

As our business grew, I needed to make sure that I upgraded our corporate talent, raising the level of the group of people who were surrounding me. What I found is that at the end of the day, it doesn't matter who you are, how old you are, where you went to school, how you were raised, or what gender you are. Anybody should be able to pick up this book and have it function as a valuable tool for either their entrance into or their evolution through the business world.

The fact is that it isn't terribly complicated, and if it is, something's wrong. Dumb it down. Make it easy. Simplify it. That's what I learned from the book that taught me the most: *How to Win Friends and Influence People*, by Dale Carnegie. It was originally published in 1936, it's still in print, and generations continue to learn from it.

Take it from me, a kid who graduated at the very bottom of his high school class. Making business success complicated doesn't improve it. The KISS (Keep It Simple, Sister) method continues to hold water. This book is designed to provide a completely understandable version of business, which means it won't be talking over your head.

If you have read many of these types of books, you know that most don't detail actionable steps but deal in theory. They don't give you the what-to-dos; they just talk in circles, in case studies, in things that don't even apply anymore. By contrast, what I'm giving you in the following pages is practical stuff. No brain surgery.

Whether you take *the secret is YOU* as a whole or break down each chapter, it's going to come back to one thing: Do you really have the mindset to be a CEO, the mentality to excel as an entrepreneur? Because that's what this book is going to challenge you to do.

Take notes, because I'm going to tell you all you need to know to be your own business owner and boss. I won't ask you to do anything that I wouldn't do. I think that serving others is the greatest thing you can be asked to do in this world, and I hope it's something you'll be taking away from the narrative adventure you're about to embark on.

I've always prided myself on being the hardest-charging person in the room. You may outshine me for a while, but you'll never outwork me. Having that work ethic ultimately pays dividends that make me or you or anyone else stand out. It's all about persistence and determination. Give me the person who wants it the most, every time.

I was never the brightest student in the classroom or the biggest dude on the football field, to put it mildly. I was a five-foot-nine kid who wasn't as fast or as talented as everyone else. I always had to work harder. But I never let that stop me.

The fact that I am dyslexic didn't prevent me from earning a high school diploma and getting accepted into a good college close to home. I pushed the envelope with every nerve in my body, and I still do. I don't have any choice. I still battle the dyslexia every day. It isn't something you overcome. You just live with it and (hopefully) learn to adapt.

No matter what your ultimate goal is, you need to carry an attitude of never giving up. Repetition is at the heart of it all. As Zig Ziglar is fond of saying, it's the mother of learning, the father of action, and the architect of accomplishment. It's so important that I've based an entire chapter in this book around it.

You'll also understand after reading *the secret is YOU* that I see myself more as a head coach who has built a remarkable team than simply a motivator. I prefer to inspire by example. This also precludes the perception of "mansplaining." The answer isn't to lecture people to death but to find and hire those who know more than I do to fill essential roles.

I'm incredibly proud of the corporate culture we have instilled at our headquarters in downtown Cincinnati, as well as of the thousands of independent consultants around the globe who have taught me so much. But to appreciate this book, you won't need to come in with any particular knowledge, nor will there be any quiz at the end. Your job as a reader is simply to take it all in, assess its value for your own life, and then find ways to effectively apply it.

Maybe you're someone who has always wanted to have their own business but has been stumped about how to get started. Maybe you're someone who has never considered having their own business but you feel like now is the right time to develop a plan. Maybe you're already a Pure Romance consultant and looking to raise your level of success. Or maybe you're one of our customers who has enjoyed attending the parties and using our products, and you're hoping to take things to the next level as a consultant.

What you will get in *the secret is YOU* is a road map for being proactive rather than reactive and living your life by design, not by default. It's a primer dedicated to teaching you how to face down the obstacles keeping you from success, and the best way to commit to the process while detaching from the outcome.

However, this book isn't about buzz terms but experiencing a whole new career reality that will help you plan your financial future and supply you with the tools necessary to become a successful entrepreneur. Along the way, I'll be sharing with you some essential survival skills I developed as well as the story of my own journey, which has had more than its share of trials and tribulations.

I'll also reveal some of my favorite business anecdotes and recommendations.

What makes me qualified for this task? I was able to scale Pure Romance to become the world's largest woman-to-woman direct seller of relationship-enhancement and intimacy products, including sex toys; bath, beauty, and cosmetic products; creams, lubricants, and massage oils; lingerie; and bedroom accessories. That's why.

But reading this book shouldn't be like poring over a textbook. I want you to have some fun not only while absorbing its message but also as you implement its ideas, because if you aren't enjoying it, there's no point. We don't live long enough not to revel in every step of this adventure.

I wish each of you all the success you can dream of. If my words play a small part in helping you thrive, you will have left me richly rewarded.

Thanks for riding shotgun with me on the journey.

Now...let's go make it happen—together.

# CHAPTER 1

# Humble Beginnings

FADE IN: Approaching a bus stop near my house in Milford, Ohio

THE YEAR: 1987

CHARACTERS: Mo (age twelve), a bully, and my mother

And...action!

"Hey, look! Here comes the sex toy lady's kid!"

"The what?" I wonder.

"We know who your mom is! She was on the radio last night talking about dildos. She's the Dildo Lady!"

Dildos? The Dildo Lady?

The kid who had just pointed and accused me of being something I didn't completely understand was somewhat older and considerably bigger than I was. I pretty much knew this wasn't going to end well. He was in the middle of the sidewalk and taunting me as I approached the bus stop, shouting what I perceived to be an insult, insinuating my mother was some kind of hooker.

"No, she isn't!" I yelled back.

In no time at all, punches started flying. I realized that I'd probably get my butt kicked, but this was about family pride. Nobody talked about my mom like that.

Fast-forward an hour or so. I was sitting in the middle school principal's office waiting for the woman whose honor I'd just defended to arrive. When she did, it was clear she wanted answers.

"What happened?" she asked in her "This had better be good" voice.

"He called you the Dildo Lady," I explained, my voice quiet, my head low. "He said you were on the radio last night talking about sex toys."

Mom nodded and sat down beside me. "I see."

The tone of my mother's answer told me that she wasn't ready for that. It was going to be slightly more complicated than she'd anticipated.

"Well, Chris," she continued, "let me tell you something." She swallowed hard. "My job is to help parents stay together. Couples need to learn how to connect, and I'm an educator. I educate women about how to keep their relationship fun."

Mind you, I didn't entirely grasp what she was telling me. You know, I was twelve. Yet it was nonetheless revealing that she was speaking to a kid whose father had abandoned the family. Besides, I knew that listening well here was going to help get me out of the potential grounding on the horizon.

"I'm trying to help other families stay together," Mom assured me. "The reality is, they're communication tools."

The whole incident left me frustrated and confused. But that said, I don't think I'd ever had greater respect for my mother than I did in that moment. It was also the first time I'd had any insight into what Mom's job was in fact really all about.

"Oh yeah, just one more thing," Mom added. "If any other kid gives you a hard time like this boy did, ever again, you just let me know. I'll be more than happy to let you bring in his parents' sales receipts, and you can put them on the bulletin board at school for everyone to see."

Little did I know then that I would one day be on the same path as my mom, helping to give women empowerment and independence over both their business and sexual lives. It's safe to say this was the last place I thought I'd ever wind up.

And...scene!

# Humble Beginnings

\* \* \*

Yep, somehow I was the kid of the lady who sold sex toys. It isn't a handle you generally wear with pride as an aspiring jock in Middle America.

As far back as I can remember, athletics was my passion, my desire, my life's purpose. I played every sport there was, and I played to win. I played baseball. I played basketball. I played soccer. Starting in the seventh grade, I played football.

I always thought I would be a football coach when I grew up. But things don't always turn out the way we expect them to, do they? I certainly couldn't envision that I'd become the President and CEO of a company selling adult toys that was launched by my mother, Patty Brisben.

After I was born in Naperville, Illinois, my earliest years were spent growing up in the Cincinnati suburb of Milford on the Little Miami River, a community of about 6,800 that's located seventeen miles from downtown Cincy. I attended Milford Junior High and then Archbishop Moeller High School, better known as just plain Moeller. It's a private, all-male, Catholic college-prep school in the burbs. You know the kind.

Patty and my dad divorced when I was five, and things got really tough in all kinds of ways. It was 1980. Dad was twenty-seven. From what I would find out later, my father's primary issue when he walked out the door was that he wanted to be with someone more successful. He claimed that Patty never looked good when he arrived. He wanted that kind of Stepford wife who was going to be there and make sure dinner was cooked and also, you know, have a sexy gown on when he came home. That was never going to be her.

From that moment, Dad rarely came into my life throughout my childhood and adolescence. I would see him maybe at Christmas and one other time during the year, and that was about it. It stayed that way into college.

Meanwhile, Patty was working for four pediatricians, earning all of $4.25 an hour. As a single mom, she had to work her butt off to put food on the table. She did everything she could to guide and support us, help us with our homework, and be *present*. But there was only one of her and four of us, so it was tough.

At first, it was just me and my brother Nick, who is two and a half years younger. Two years later, Patty married Bob Brisben and had two more kids back-to-back: my brother Matt and my sister Lauren. About a year later, beginning in 1983—when I was eight—she started working part-time for a company called F.U.N. Parties, whose consultants hosted parties selling intimacy products and such.

Patty and my stepdad were barely able to make ends meet. They raised us in a bi-level house in Milford until I was a freshman in high school. The parties took up more and more of Patty's time, to the point where she was working twenty to twenty-five nights a month.

Yet the truth is that I never felt like a latchkey kid. Either Patty or my stepdad was there, or we had a babysitter. It was also important to Patty to get us on the bus for school in the morning and off the bus at the end of the school day. She was a great mom in every way, struggling to be our rock and refusing to apologize for doing what she had to do to give us a more comfortable life.

Patty's reason for being gone so much was indeed to better us as a family. I don't ever want to say she was an absentee mom, because she wasn't. She juggled everything and attended all of my athletic events. Even if she wasn't there for the full game, she always made it for part. On the other hand, it was true that some nights she'd throw a twenty-dollar bill on the counter and say, "Hey, get some Domino's tonight for dinner."

It wasn't just that Patty loved making money. Working the parties also sent her self-esteem soaring. It changed the way she saw herself and how she viewed the world.

Patty taught me all about hard work. She was trying to build a business and maintain a growing family at the same time, and it was clear how difficult that was. At the same time, she never complained. She just stepped up and did it. She was out late and up early. Her energy never flagged.

As the big brother of this family, I often had the responsibility of taking care of my three siblings while Mom was away even when we had a babysitter—making sure they all did their homework, they were in bed on time, that kind of thing. I was forced to mature and learn self-sufficiency at a younger age than most. Plus, I couldn't depend on my working mother, my missing father, or my stepfather to make me happy. In hindsight, I think this independence helped prepare me for life more fully.

I've often thought about what impact my upbringing may have had on my adult mindset. I know for sure that I took a protective interest in my family—looking out to guard against the tarnishing of Patty's reputation and taking pains to shield my brothers and sister from anything the community may have been dishing about the woman raising us.

Maybe it's this same idea of looking after my younger sibs that stays with me today in taking a paternal interest in the women who work with Pure Romance (and, by extension, for themselves). I know that I put myself into Patty's headspace and identified with her struggle. I do everything in my power to help our people achieve financial independence and avoid the insecurities that dogged Patty as a single mother during her transition to sales.

It wasn't really until I was a young teenager when it fully hit me that what Patty did for a living wasn't as socially acceptable as if she were, say, a teacher or nurse or stay-at-home mom. I wasn't ashamed at all, but it did leave me feeling more vigilant about outside observations. I knew that she loved us and was doing what she was doing in her job to support us, and that was enough for me. At the same time, we were living in a conservative enclave, and with that came judgment.

Yet it was in school that I faced my greatest personal challenge, struggling like crazy academically. Oh man, did I struggle. The thing is, I wanted to be a good student so badly. I grew discouraged because teachers kept telling me that I was slow, that I was this, that I was that. I just kept getting labeled as being scholastically challenged, and it sucked.

It all came to a head in my fourth-grade year. I got put in the slow reading group at Pleasant Hill Elementary in Cincinnati. Things went downhill from there. They finally called Patty in and told her, "We need to hold Chris back."

Yes, I flunked the fourth grade. Flunked. The. Fourth. Grade. How can you flunk the fourth grade? I figured out a way. It was all about the reading. After that, I kept getting put in the lower-level group even though I knew in my head, on some level, that I wasn't meant to be there. It was incredibly frustrating.

I indeed wound up repeating the academic year. Patty was determined to get to the bottom of it. Once a week and sometimes twice, she would drive me to a tutoring facility in Dayton (about an hour from my house), where I'd watch a ball move back and forth for forty-five minutes. The theory was that this ball would train my brain and improve my reading, though I'm not sure how much it actually helped.

What stuck with me during this difficult time was Patty's steadfast commitment to helping me become a better student. She had always been a taskmaster, which is why it was kind of miraculous that she never gave me a hard time about my test results and grades. As busy as she was, Patty made sure to pledge that time to helping my reading. Every single week.

Athletics was my refuge through it all. Playing team sports was a revelation for me, and I was really good at it. I loved being part of a group and knowing the role I played in its success. I lived for the camaraderie. I loved the competition (both within myself to get better, and against the other team). I loved the way it motivated me to become my best. I loved the stage of team sports and playing for something bigger than myself.

I love everything about sports to this day, and one way you can tell is my liberal use of sports analogies in my daily work life. Back in high school, it was the sports world and my interaction with coaches that helped shape me as a man. The coaches were, in hindsight, my real father figures.

Sports is what got me respect and advancement, in school and with my peers. I was one of the standouts in junior high at Milford. My stepdad had gone to Moeller, and I remember going to my first football game there and seeing ten thousand people packed into the stands—for a high school game! It made me think, "Wow. I want to come here." It was the same thing when I watched a basketball game there, with all the team spirit and alumni excitement.

My football coach at Moeller, Tim Shira, quickly grew to become my primary male role model. He had a significant impact on my development as both an athlete and a human being, instilling along with Patty a powerful work ethic in me. He told me that I could *be* something, and he helped me understand the positive outcomes that emerge from hard work.

Moeller was a place that was, for a football athlete, all about practice and preparation and playing the role you were meant to play.

I was a defensive back and punt returner, and in part because of Coach Shira, I would stay on the field for an hour after formal practice had ended and everyone else had gone home, to perfect my technique and execution. I would take literally one hundred catches of his punts every day and run them back. I was pretty good at it, but if I wanted to be the best—and I did—I needed to put in the time. Coach understood that and made sure I had the opportunity. It was all about working the process, punt after punt. After punt.

*Lesson: commit to the process and turn practice into habit.*

My sports lessons would stay with me into my personal and career lives as an adult. I learned, for instance, that there is no "I" in "team." But the even greater teachings came out of failure, namely as a student.

Again, it wasn't the lack of effort that made my academic life so miserable in school; it was circumstances beyond my control (until I was finally able to control them). Because I graduated pretty much at the bottom of my high school class—167 out of 169—I had to beg to get into college. I mean *literally* beg.

Yet I was more determined than ever to get accepted into a good school. The problem was that my GPA hovered around a 2.2. Plus, now it was my senior year, and things were getting serious. I started making my college visits, and that's when I got my second SAT score back after having tallied just a 630 the first time. Unfortunately, I needed a 700 or above to get into college and play football.

Now it was February, and the clock was seriously ticking.

It was about this time that Patty was made aware of my dilemma. She hooked me up with the Sylvan Learning Center, to see if they might have any answers to help me finally get up to speed on the SAT on my third try. The lady there evaluated me and fortunately thought to ask, "Have you ever been tested for dyslexia?"

"What's that?" I asked.

"Well," she said, "it's a learning disability. Have you ever been tested?"

"No."

The woman tested me and—of course—I had dyslexia. The diagnosis allowed me to take the SAT with extra time allowances. Her theory was that the time limits themselves were getting me too worked up. I still wasn't convinced that extra time was going to make a difference, but it was obviously more than worth a shot.

Mount Union College (later the University of Mount Union) in Alliance, Ohio, a small liberal arts school, was one of the campuses that I'd toured around this time, in early '94. I had no intention of going to an NCAA Division III school, which this was. I was all about landing a spot playing football for a much more prestigious Division I college. Unfortunately, I was running out of options.

Greg King was in charge of admissions at Mount Union. He recognized that I wasn't anything close to a model student. But he liked my athleticism and enthusiasm, and promised that he and the football coaching staff would work to get me admitted if I scored at least 700 on that elusive SAT.

I took the test again, this time without the same time constraints. It was now March. I called Greg daily, religiously, to check in, just to say, "Hey, Greg, it's me again. Anything else I can do? Anything you need from me?" Just to make sure that he knew how seriously I was taking this. After all, he was really my only option at this point, my last hope.

In June, I got word that I'd finally sufficiently raised my number when my two best scores from my second and third tests were combined and averaged. I'd come in at 730.

I was finally able to exhale and rejoice, "I'm going to college!" I was super excited, being the first one in my family to actually attend.

Going to Mount Union changed the whole trajectory of my life. That I'm sure about.

I was still immature when I walked through the MU doors, still really kind of a boy. But I had to grow up fast. Here's why: as soon as I entered the school as a freshman, Patty and my stepdad, Bob, went through a really horrible divorce. There was infidelity. There was embezzlement. There were just a whole lot of things going on, and I was four hours away from home as it all went down.

I'd always been kind of the man of the house, and I was probably still basically a mama's boy at that time. Patty was calling me every night to fill me in on what was going on. I was feeling the pain from afar while adjusting to a new school. Also, my brother Nick was facing a lot of problems himself while attending Moeller and had, in fact, just gotten kicked out. Not surprisingly, my grades veered quickly south.

I wanted to drop out. But my coach at the time convinced me that if I stayed, it would be worth it.

"You don't have to go through this alone," he reassured me. "I'll help you."

It turned out to be an especially difficult freshman year. College was much different than I expected, having my attention and focus so split. But sticking with it totally paid off, because after packing up my car and preparing to move home to help Patty and my family back in Cincinnati, everything fell into place instead. Mom really came through, sitting me down and convincing me to return and follow my own path, my own goals, and focus on my dream. By the time I got back to school, I was ready to go. Instead of being a giant change, it proved to be a tiny hiccup.

This all goes back to the fact that you always have to plan for 15 percent of your life not to go as planned, a mantra I would return to again and again in the business world.

I went on to become an all-conference defensive back in football at Mount Union, where we won back-to-back Division III National Titles in 1996 and '97. It was all based on embracing my purpose with the Purple Raiders and staying within my role for our team. Great coaches know how to bring that mentality out in their players, and I've been blessed to have amazing men leading me in athletics. Combining that teamwork and role-playing mantra I learned in high school helped me thrive in college.

This kind of athletic success also taught me that no one is interested in playing for a team that's just a one-man or one-woman show. We want to be part of a legacy, something that lives forever. There isn't a lot of glory in being the best player on an 0–15 team. The team that everyone is going to talk about is the one that goes 15–0, plays their butts off, and wins as a unit. These are the guys who will get together years later and reminisce, "You know what, man? We built something unbelievable, and we did it together."

Sports was where I learned that the strongest players help make even the weakest links contribute meaningfully to the cause. It also doesn't hurt to have guts. When I was playing high school football on special teams and returning punts, "fair catch" was not really in my vocabulary. If you advanced even one yard after the catch, that was yardage—and if you had to take a brutal hit to get it, you did.

I didn't set any academic records at MU—and in fact I fell twelve units short of graduation—but things worked out well on the football field. What stands out most from that experience was the honor of being mentored by my coach, Don Montgomery. The lessons I was taught by my coaches have stayed with me.

My high school teachers, however, suggested that I should consider going to tech school. Tech school! In college, fortunately, my thinking and my fortunes completely shifted. I started to believe in myself, imagining, "I can do whatever I want to do, achieve whatever I want to achieve." My mindset did a complete one-eighty.

It was actually during the summer between my junior and senior years of college that everything changed. I needed an internship, so I called Patty and told her the job had to be something that wasn't in state, that paid me, and that was outside of my major (which was secondary education, as I planned to be a football coach).

"Plus, I need to find something in forty-eight hours," I informed her.

Yes, like almost every college kid, I had been procrastinating on this, and now the situation was down to the wire.

Patty got on the phone and called a bunch of people she knew, but nothing came to fruition. She finally had to break down and call my father, who was the newly appointed COO of a publicly traded floor covering company near Atlanta called the Maxim Group. When I tell you that this was the very last person on earth Mom wanted to deal with, I mean he really was the *last* person. Patty never took him back to court when he started making more money to increase the child support from him.

She got Dad on the phone and said, "You have done nothing for this child for twenty years of his life. Nothing. This is what he needs. You *have* to do it." He told her, "Fine, he can come here and do his internship."

To make a long story fairly short, Maxim was nothing like I'd imagined. My mom had taken me to buy one khaki suit and three dress shirts to get me through. My first week was spent at a giant sewing machine making carpet, turning my shirts and suit brown with sweat and grime. See, my mom always told me you that have to dress for the part you want, not the part you have. But I had no idea I'd start out in a warehouse. It had to be 117 degrees in that place, and I wondered, "What did I sign up for?" My dad had sold this to me as an office internship, but in reality I was just sewing carpets.

Having gotten a handle on what it was like to be a factory worker, I was shifted over to merchandising, where I worked for another week. Then I got moved to the sales training side, learning how the company mentors its salespeople—also for a week.

Finally, I was put out on the road, which was easily the best time of the internship. It started with my being flown out from Atlanta to Orange County, California. It was so freakin' cool. I had never seen the Pacific Ocean, and now here I was in Southern California with the palm trees. I went on sales calls with a guy who interacted with everyone like a pro. Got to see the ocean and feel the breezes. For a kid who had never really been anywhere outside of Ohio, it was beyond fantastic.

I ended up leaving SoCal after two days and headed for another sales experience in Nebraska, then flew to Charleston, South Carolina. I remember this guy in Charleston who told me he was twenty-one. He pulled up in his white BMW and said, "Hey, jump in, we're running late."

After tossing my bags in the back, I saw that he had all these carpet samples in the trunk. We picked up some doughnuts and headed to his next store appointment, then to another one. Wherever we went, this dude owned the room. He motivated the sellers with gift cards for selling the most yardage of carpet or the highest amount. The guy was so good, he was just electric.

While dropping me off at my hotel that first day, he said, "Hey, me and a couple of buddies are going to take in a [minor league Charleston] RiverDogs ballgame. Want to come with us?" I went, and it was awesome. Feasted on hot dogs and beer. He pulled out a big wad of cash to pay for everything.

Fortified by the liquid courage, I asked him, "Hey, man, did you go to college for this?"

"No," he replied. "I just picked up this job like two years ago."

"I know this isn't a question I should ask, but I'm kind of curious: How much do you make a year?"

"Last year, I made $117,000."

This was in 1997 dollars. I couldn't believe my ears. But there was more.

"I'm on pace to take in $150,000 this year," he assured me.

"Damn" was all I could manage to say.

I had no idea this internship was going to change my career path. But it did.

Returning for my senior year of college, I went all-in to turn around my future direction. Changing majors midstream to business required a lot of academic backtracking. By the following year, I was miserable. I was still at Mount Union, only now on my victory lap fifth year. I was no longer playing football but coaching high school ball nearby in Alliance. I so badly wanted to get my life started. That's when in frustration, I called Maxim.

I'd applied there just to tell Maxim I was a semester away from graduating. But then something opened up in the merchandising department. This was in November. By December, I was back in Atlanta working full-time. They also promised to pay for my tuition at Kennesaw State University so I could finish my degree and hooked me up with a nice apartment, for which they promised to pay six months' rent.

A month after I arrived, though, the company announced the $570 million acquisition of Shaw Retail, and I was sent to Chicago to take a position as district manager. On the day I arrived, the regional vice president resigned and, at twenty-two, I suddenly found myself in charge of a region that did $29 million in annual sales for a company called Carpetland USA, which my dad had helped build back in the eighties. Really serendipitous, right?

Well talk about trial by fire. Fresh out of college and without having finished, I had a lot of people reporting to me. I got a crash course in supervision and balance sheets and was fortunate to report to Wayde Triska, who taught me more than I can adequately convey here. Wayde took me under his wing and helped me thrive in what could otherwise have been a disastrous situation.

But, I mean, think about it. I was barely old enough to drink, and I had to read financial statements and understand cash flow for a large and growing company, observe employee performance to learn who was and wasn't reaching their targets, and fire people who weren't producing.

The good news was, I took a region that had been severely in the red and moved it to a break-even point, quickly raising my profile in the corporate offices. I had all kinds of autonomy. I could do anything I wanted to. It was great. Chicago was growing on me, too.

Then they called me back to headquarters in Atlanta and offered me a position with a new subsidiary start-up inside Maxim. They were going to sell carpet and home furnishings on this thing called the internet, and planned to make me director of merchandising on all floor coverings, window treatments, paint, and everything else sold online in this new division called Everything Décor.

This was a very early foray into online sales. Now, of course, this job would have been a snap. Back then, e-commerce was new and untested. Big companies were still trying to figure out how to harness this potential resource to increase sales.

I saw it as an awesome opportunity, an exciting new venture into uncharted waters. Plus, they wanted to double my salary as well as give me a $50,000 cash signing bonus and $100,000 in stock—which would ultimately never be worth a penny. More on that in a moment.

Companies had a lot of fears then about making their product pricing so public for their competitors, so I heard my fair share of "no." In the early phases of internet commerce, only the big companies could afford to develop the technology infrastructure to sell online. I mean, Amazon was only six years old and years from profitability when we launched Everything Décor.

The challenge was selling people on something they had never done before, convincing them there was opportunity in this new sales channel early in its development. What I learned in the job was determination and tenacity. I'd make calls, send letters, craft emails, do whatever was necessary to get meetings and build the business.

It was thrilling. Here I was, almost twenty-five years old, and I was meeting with the CEO of Sherwin-Williams, the CEO of Benjamin Moore, the CEO of Sealy—the top of the top. It really helped me hone my skills in dealing with that C-suite type of mentality.

I had been doing this for about six months when the Securities and Exchange Commission finished an investigation into the parent company (Maxim) in June 2000. I was working on a tile spreadsheet that day, and I remember sitting there when all of a sudden I heard the following announcement: "Stop what you are doing and take your hands off your keyboard! Grab your stuff and exit the building immediately!"

Looking around, I continued typing, thinking this was somehow funny. A woman came up behind me and warned, "If you take another stroke on that keyboard, I will arrest and handcuff you. This is an

FBI raid. It is *not* a *joke!* Grab your personal belongings and leave the building—now!"

Clearly, the FBI had no sense of humor.

This was the craziest experience of my life. It was also the end of Everything Décor and my burgeoning career at the Maxim Group.

The good news is that it didn't take me long to land another job offer. This time it was a position at the headquarters of tile manufacturer Casa Tile, in St. Louis. The plan was for me to spend half of the year at the company headquarters and (more enticingly) half the year in Bologna, Italy. For an Italian guy like me, what could be better than that?

I was all set to accept the job when Patty called.

"Chris," she began, "what would you think about joining me at Pure Romance? I want you to help me grow this company."

Me: "Maybe I can come back and just help you for a few months, put together a business plan, start helping to expand your footprint?"

Patty: "That would be great."

Me: "What can you afford to pay me, Mom?"

Patty: "How's $24,000?"

Me: "Horrible."

Patty: "When can you start?"

Me: "Uh, now?"

Oh, well. Goodbye, Italy. Hello again, Milford.

But the bottom line was that I had a rare opportunity to repay Patty after all she had done for me growing up. I thought that's all it would be—helping her with a future business plan and then moving on to continue my own career.

That is not, of course, how things turned out. Not even close.

## Takeaways

- Now is the time to stop putting labels on yourself and others. If I would have listened to my teachers, and if my mother would have listened to society, we would have remained paralyzed by self-doubt and negativity. This is why you need to listen only to your own internal GPS. The opinions of others will only lead you astray.

- You are the rainmaker, the dream creator. Now is the time to think about the labels and limitations you put on yourself and drop them away forever. Remember that you determine your outputs. Don't let things you can't change affect the way you grow and do business.

- Your attitude is paramount. Exactly 100 percent of your success is tied to your attitude, in all areas of your life. Attitude is what leads to hard work, and it's all about the team. You need to know your role and how you best contribute to the team. Attitude is what determines how you attack a problem and how you fill your role. Attitude, attitude, attitude.

## CHAPTER 2

# Facing Down the Obstacles

In opting not to accept an offer from a tile company that would put me in Italy for half of the year, and instead help my mom take her direct-sales business for bedroom toys and lubricants to the next level, I was choosing family over money, Ohio over Italy, home over adventure. I was putting assisting the woman who put me through college over making my own way.

Mind you, after spending time living in Atlanta and Chicago, I could not imagine going back to residing in my hometown. I'd tasted corporate travel and the big-business life, and I was intrigued. I wanted more of that. With the Maxim Group, I had been working in a gigantic office building with a great atrium, a food court, a chef on-site. I'd grown a little bit spoiled.

Yet I figured it couldn't hurt to sit down with Patty and check out her books to see where things stood.

"I feel like my business is doing great," she told me, "but I just can't completely scale it. I can't seem to break through the numbers."

After looking at her balance sheet and profit and loss statement, I was impressed. Patty knew she had something, but up to this point she had been unable to focus on growth. That would be my role.

"I know it's pretty good," she told me, "but I think I should be doing better, and I can't do it by myself. I need your help."

With all her parties, Patty was bringing in something in the low six figures annually. It was barely enough to pay her and a handful of staff—and hire me, if I'd accept $2,000 a month. But Patty laid on the guilt: "Look, here's the deal: I *really* need to get this business out there. I sent you to college. That was my business plan. Now, I need you to help me figure out how to grow this thing."

Yes, it was time to scale it. I saw it as my role from the start to work *on* the business while my mother worked *in* the business. Patty understood that I didn't know anything about the products she was selling, but it didn't matter. I could see from the profit and loss statement that there was tremendous potential for growth and a significant need for expansion. Plus, my circumstances at the time—I was an unmarried twenty-five-year-old guy with no kids, no ties—convinced me I should take a chance.

By the same token, I wasn't really looking to get into the family business. I thought of it as Mom's "play business." I'd already worked for a publicly traded company. I'd just be with Mom for a couple of months, help square her financials, put together a marketing plan, and move on. No way would I be staying in this gig longer than necessary.

When I came onboard in August 2000, I was the sixth full-time employee at Pure Romance. Today, we have well over a hundred people in our corporate headquarters in Cincinnati. Their role is to support the women in the field with marketing materials and product training, and the employees at our warehouse to ensure that products get to our consultants all over the world. But that all was a long way off in 2000.

On day one, I was a guy without his own office in a 1,500-square-foot warehouse getting paid $24k. My task was to market the business, grow our consultant numbers (we had about three hundred at the time), and expand the organization.

(So you can better understand what I'm talking about, a Pure Romance consultant is a sexual health and wellness brand affiliate. She markets and sells our bath, beauty, and wellness products, along with our premier line of intimacy products, at in-home parties, virtual parties, or online through her personal Pure Romance website.)

At the time, I knew we had to convince more consultants to sign on—but how?

This question was racing through my head one day shortly after I signed on as I turned my car onto Interstate 275, which is our loop. Suddenly this ad popped on the radio: "Come meet Felipe, the photographer to the stars, at the Holiday Inn on Route 42 and be our next Guess jeans model! Today only! For ninety-nine dollars at the Holiday Inn, get your picture taken by L.A.'s famous photographer...and you might be our next Guess jeans model and see your way to Hollywood!"

I was listening to this and thinking, "Man, would somebody really pay ninety-nine bucks for the slim chance to be a Guess jeans model?" All I knew was that I had to get over there and find out. So, I flipped my car around and drove back to Sharonville from Milford. I exited the freeway. There was a McDonald's at the off-ramp. I rounded the corner past the Mickey D's and it was like, "Oh my God!" Packed. Beyond. There had to be 250 people lined up there. I got out and started talking to the people in line, and they were insisting, "Yeah, I want to be the next Guess jeans model."

Now I was thinking, "This is *it*." I stayed up all night. Probably drank eight cups of coffee. Came into work the next morning and said to Patty, "Mom, I know exactly what we're going to do. We're going to run ads that say, 'Come meet Patty Brisben! Take the next steps in making your dreams come true! For ninety-nine dollars, own and operate your own Pure Romance business! Come meet Patty at the Sheraton Westport Plaza in St. Louis! Ladies, at 7 p.m., the party starts here!'"

Patty replied, "That is the worst f-ing idea that I think I've ever heard. Why the heck would anyone want to meet *me*?"

I told her, "Mom, this industry needs a voice—and you're it. You're articulate. You have strong convictions about women's health and having ownership of their bodies. They need that, and they require somebody strong enough to stand up against those who think we're a pornography company."

Reluctantly, Patty agreed. The idea was that we'd have marketing events where the women would meet Patty, see how fabulous she was, sign on to our company, meet other successful consultants, take one of our product kits, and start planning their own parties.

I mean, what could possibly go wrong—besides everything?

For that first trip to St. Louis, we took a giant gamble and sank $30,000 into marketing it when we had only $33,000 in our bank account at the time. We ran a ton of advertising and promotions. Why St. Louis? Because it was the second most conservative city in the area. (Cincinnati was number one.) My theory was that if we could make it in Cincinnati and St. Louis, we could make it anywhere.

We were set up in a nice suburban shopping center, and Patty was doing great on all these radio interviews plugging it. We'd driven a U-Haul to St. Louis packed with a bundle of our product kits. I was stoked. We were ready. My biggest concern was how swamped we would be by the giant group of women who were sure to descend on us, and if we could handle them all.

And then *no one* showed up. *Nada. Zip.*

Not a single person.

I cannot tell you how shocked and devastated I was, but I'm sure you have some idea. I remember thinking, "Oh my God. We're screwed!" But we still had one more day in St. Louis, and we picked up and moved to a nice downtown hotel close to the baseball stadium. I remember dropping to my knees that morning, begging, "Please, *somebody* show up."

But there we were throughout the morning. Nobody. Noon, still no one. One o'clock, crickets.

Finally, at two o'clock, the first person in two days showed up. Big sigh of relief. By the end of the day, ten women had come by, and two of them wound up becoming consultants. We were excited. We were high-fiving. At the time, we were adding two new consultants a month, so I saw this as a big success.

Briefly.

Unfortunately, given our radio advertising purchase, we had just plunked down $15,000 per consultant, not including our travel expenses.

Not a terribly sound business model.

We went out to celebrate that night at the Italian landmark Tony's in downtown St. Louis with a pair of our experienced consultants—B.J. Jones and Kelly Anson—who were traveling with us. I was afraid I might exceed the dollar limit on my credit card. After the check came, I sneaked into the men's room to call the bank on my cell phone. We were just barely under the limit, avoiding a huge dose of embarrassment.

By the end of the night, though, I was convinced we had made the biggest mistake of our lives and it was going to bankrupt the company. There was no way we could travel from city to city recruiting consultants at $15,000 a pop.

Now what? *Now what?*

Then came the next morning.

I got into the office at about seven. By nine thirty, the phone started ringing off the hook. I was thinking people were trying to fax in their orders and the machine was out or the voice recorder wasn't picking up calls, so now people were just calling in left and right.

Finally, I decided to pick up the phone.

"Hi, this is Chris. Thank you so much for calling Pure Romance."

The woman on the other end said, "Hi. I'd like to sign up with your company."

"Wow!" I replied. "Awesome. Where are you from?"

"St. Louis."

"Great, and how did you hear about us? Was it on the radio?"

"No."

"Oh, well then, did you come to our event?"

"No."

"Oh. Then how did you hear about us?"

My curiosity was off the charts.

"Well," the woman said, "my husband was out picking up a few things for breakfast this morning, and he brought home a copy of the [St. Louis] *Post-Dispatch* [newspaper]. On the front page of the Style section was this story, 'The New Tupperware of the 2000s,' and it named your company."

Yes, one of the ten women who came to our event turned out to be a lifestyle reporter for the *Post-Dispatch*!

This lady went on, "Yeah, and this article said you were empowering women to make more decisions in the bedroom, and this was the new party plan of the century. I want to be a part of that."

I practically dropped the phone. There was no possible way I could have paid for that kind of endorsement. As soon as this article landed, it gave us instant credibility. Over the next week, we signed up fifty brand-new people. And that was the model Patty and I took on the road for the next three years.

After we were done in St. Louis, I was like, "I think we have something here. This could work." But oh my God, it was a battle. Every day, there was an argument. I get it now, of course. It's tough when an entrepreneur (Patty) hands her baby over to an operator (me). Plus, in my mid-twenties I was a bull in a china shop: "Get out of my way! We'll figure it out on the fly! Let's do this thing!" I would fly off the handle and do battle at the drop of a hat. Patty fought almost everything I ever tried.

Also, Patty was a perfectionist to the nth degree. She was all about, "It has to be done *this* way." Meanwhile, I was about progress: "It's close enough; let's move on."

But we both wanted the same thing: for this business to explode. So, we figured out a way to coexist, because intellectually, if not emotionally, we understood that we were perfect puzzle pieces that fit together. And we had that familial level of trust.

Patty was an expert on the product and party side. That was her baby, and I left it alone. But how do you scale it? How do you make it duplicable? How do you market it? How do you spread the word far and wide? That's where I came in. We had to put all of those things in place, including the branding. The products were not all branded to fit in a collection. They were pretty much a mishmash. The catalog was still printed in black and white, on yellowish paper.

With our traveling marketing blueprint born, Patty and I packed up the U-Haul with product kits in the back and went from city to city all around the Midwest, hosting open houses and doing radio, TV, and newspaper interviews everywhere we landed.

We would start building in a market and then, three months later, return to train the group of new consultants. Each of them was charged with her own Pure Romance party business, and on the road our mantra was to provide a safe environment for women to come learn about an exciting business opportunity and discover our products. Our strategy was to impart to women the idea that they could take control over their sexuality and, at the same time, bring in another income stream for their families.

Was it a home run right away? Not even close. We didn't make any money for the first eight years. You have to keep pouring what you make back into a company to raise it to the next level.

Our model would be, say, spending $50,000 to open a market with various events and media. Then we'd plunk down another $50,000 over two years in training and development. That market might produce only $100,000 in business during that couple of years, so we were treading water for a while. We had to be okay with not recouping our investment in most markets for maybe five or six years, understanding that when the payoff came, it would come big. That's just what you do when you play the long game.

As tough as the U-Haul years were, in many ways they were great, because we had endless hours of conversation that taught me my mother's business. I learned how she thought about things, her inspiration, her struggles, her mindset.

The reason we succeeded is we never looked at Pure Romance as a short-term play, which is what I see way too many business owners doing today. Even McDonald's isn't fast enough for a lot of people. Too many are looking to make a quick buck at the expense of the longer term, and everyone's seeking instant gratification that tells them how well they're doing. That can prove paralyzing, because you're not going to like a lot of what you hear.

I was determined that we were going to pay our dues and that it would produce dividends in the end. And it has. But it was a lengthy, slow grind getting there.

*Consultant Spotlight:*
**Melissa Messenger**

*(Lives in Sobieski, Wisconsin; twenty years with Pure Romance—for eighteen of those, using it as her primary gig. Signed up at one of our original road events in 2002.)*

"I love the self-confidence that being a Pure Romance consultant has given me. I love that it allows me such a flexible schedule and the opportunity to set my family up with a financially comfortable future.

"I regularly fall back in love with my business and share what I've learned with other women. I also regularly challenge myself to step outside of my comfort zone and grow as a business owner. As my business evolves, the goals change.

"The pandemic reinforced my gratitude for this business. Having the capacity to pivot and do much of my work online has been a godsend.

"Working at Pure Romance has opened my mind to see that bedroom toys and intimacy products are normal. We offer things to keep a two-year, a twenty-year, or a forty-year marriage fun, fresh, and exciting."

Starting on September 21, 2000, Patty and I towed a U-Haul behind us for the first year, then pulled a full-on trailer for the two years after that—well into 2003. We carried boxes of product starter kits, were on the road constantly, and we struggled. We didn't stay in the nicest hotels. We didn't have Google Maps or GPS in the vehicle. We were folding and taping boxes and loading and unloading the U-Haul to set up for our open houses in hotels. We're talking way, way old school. We were appearing on the radio at 3 a.m. if they would have us, driving to the next town, setting up, and doing it all over again.

Patty and I laid down a map of the Midwest with Cincinnati in the middle, took a piece of string, and made a circle with seven hours of driving distance in every direction. (Seven hours was the maximum that Patty could be in the car without completely melting down.)

Charlotte, North Carolina, was beyond the seven-hour limitation, but it was worth going there, because we signed up another fifty consultants in that single city.

The money kept pouring in—and out. In 2001, we spent close to $1 million on radio advertising alone. I knew that commute times were increasing and therefore people were spending more time in their cars... listening to the radio. That made it a logical buy.

However, given our product category, it wasn't easy to sell ourselves to a national radio audience. We were fortunate to work with Clear Channel and its president, Randy Michaels, to run a daytime campaign in exchange for that million bucks. We wound up getting our investment returned, and then some. But that isn't to say the outlay didn't lead to a lot of sleepless nights for me, since we didn't actually have the money in the bank when we spent it.

What we did was hustle. We wrote our own radio copy and tested out the market receptivity in our home area of southern Ohio. We also persuaded stations to feature Patty to the tune of 150 interviews a year. We turned the Federal Communication Commission guidelines on language and content into a fun challenge, often using double entendres and euphemisms to ensure compliance.

It was fortunate that Patty was so articulate and quick on her feet. If she hadn't been, the interviews could have gone downhill in a hurry. Instead, she was informative, colorful, and entertaining, and her personality not only helped promote our company but smoothed out any potential issues with those who didn't like what we were doing.

Not that we didn't run into plenty of obstacles along the way. Our uphill battle surrounded the fact that too many people had a negative view of who we were, what we did, and how we operated because of our product category.

People still use religion to label intimacy products taboo. We had to hire a First Amendment attorney for that reason. Let me just say, there are certain areas in the country that have unique (and unnecessarily restrictive) laws when it comes to sexually oriented products.

The state of Alabama, for example, has banned the possession or sale of so-called sex toys since 1998. Texas, too, had forbidden the sale of most such products (punishable by as much as two years in jail) until the law was overturned in 2008). And in 2009, Sandy Springs, Georgia, passed an ordinance forbidding the distribution of "any device designed or marketed as useful primarily for the stimulation of human genital organs."

Patty almost got arrested once in Cincinnati. It was 1985, during the early days of her work with F.U.N. Parties. She was doing a big event at the Holiday Inn in Sharonville, Ohio, about sixteen miles from Cincy. It was coincidentally the same hotel where Felipe, the photographer to the stars, would later be searching for the next Guess model. She was in a meeting room promoting Valentine's Day gifts. I was ten at the time and was with my siblings swimming in the pool. It was like a staycation for us before that term was invented.

One man walked in, approached Patty, and started in, "Hey, where are all of the dirty things? Show me those." The toys would never be laid out on a table in plain sight but were displayed in a separate shopping area. Meanwhile, this guy—who was on the older side—came back three or four more times. He finally antagonized her with, "Hey, so if I buy this, can you show me how it works?" Patty replied, "No, but your significant other can show you." The guy insisted, "No, I want *you* to show me."

Of course, the guy was trying to entrap her for soliciting prostitution, and Patty wasn't taking the bait. It turns out he was an undercover cop. Later that night, a female officer and a detective came by, took her into the hallway, and read her her Miranda rights. But after the video was reviewed, it was quickly determined that she didn't break the law, and that was it.

I also remember the day I came home from football practice in high school and there were four people carrying signs in front of our house protesting what Patty was selling—as if they were making a statement she was going to take to heart. It was crazy foolish. They thought she was ruining marriages and creating infidelity when in fact she was doing the opposite.

There were several conservative groups that targeted our business as salacious. One of them was called Concerned Citizens for Family Values. But the sophisticated brand we established, and our reputation, gave them no opening to come after us.

It wasn't as if we were telling people to go out and share their body with someone who wasn't their partner if they were in a committed relationship. We were instead helping them to enhance what they already had or rebuild what may have been lost. Our goal with our products was to strengthen romantic bonds, and our consultants assured us (and continue to assure us) that we consistently achieve just that.

What bothers me is the ignorance people display when they have their own interpretation of what someone does without bothering to sit across the table from the person and talk it out. As I always tell our people, you're not there to win the argument; you're there to have a tennis match. You're there to keep the conversation going. The longer you do, the more chances there are to get your point across.

I remember one woman in Lexington, Kentucky. We were running some TV and radio spots there, and she really wanted them off the air. She was interviewed on the local news and was literally saying that we were anti-American, anti-this, anti-that. She was convinced we were going against God's laws with what we were selling.

Again, I wasn't trying to win the argument with her when I said, "You know, I appreciate your comments. I have just one question for you: Do you believe in healthy, loving relationships?" She responded, "Yes, that's what the Bible states." And I replied to her, "That's exactly what our consultants around the United States are helping people to do. They're out there working to bring down the divorce rate."

She didn't really have an answer for that, of course. But the point is that we've been able to flip the switch on the narrative around these products in a highly conservative area of the country. That's something I'm really proud of. We overcame significant social stigma, similar in a way to the one surrounding marijuana. We took intimacy products out of the trashy back of a bookstore, softened the idea of them, and made the conversation about sexual health and relationship wellness—not getting laid.

When I joined Pure Romance, I realized that we needed to add validation to what we were saying. We knew it was "normal" for people to incorporate our products into their relationships. But it would help to have an expert confirm it. That led to an affiliation with professors Debby Herbenick and Michael Reece at the Center for Sexual Health Promotion at Indiana University.

"Our research shows that sexual enhancement products help couples to address important issues in their sex lives," Professor Herbenick said in her endorsement of Pure Romance products. "For example, taking the pressure off a partner to 'give' her an orgasm—in the case of vibrators—and easing sexual discomfort or pain—in the case of lubricants. Plus, the parties themselves provide important, comfortable spaces for women to learn about their bodies, explore their sexuality, and feel a sense of 'permission' to ask questions."

Michael Krychman, a world-renowned gynecologist, the executive director of the Southern California Center for Sexual Health and Survivorship Medicine in Newport Beach, California, and a sexual health advisor for the Patty Brisben Foundation, told me, "Sexual boredom is a very big issue. The incorporation of a sexual accessory like those sold by your company goes a long way toward making things better and easier in the bedroom, particularly as we age."

All of this said, people who are uneducated still immediately go to, "Oh, you sell sex toys? You sell vibrators? You're peddling smut." This is why we've worked so hard to establish a mainstream image of class and education and have very strict guidelines. When a consultant walks into the home of a Pure Romance host, she's dressed professionally. She's there to do a job, and she has to look the part. I always say, "You're a business owner. You need to dress like one."

Also, we train our consultants to speak with articulation and authority. We don't use obscenity or slang or improper terminology. We market the products through talking about relationships and communication. It's what Patty established in creating a very safe, secure place where women can shop, ask questions, feel comfortable, and let down their hair a little bit. We also offer an option at parties to go into a private consultation room to make purchases and ask questions. Or, if you're in a virtual party on Zoom, you can go into a breakout room and say, "Hey, this is what I'm looking for."

At the core of our Pure Romance parties is the idea that people too often lose creativity when it comes to their relationships. Our consultants are like a Pinterest board for your love life. They recommend how to have a great night with products to put in play that will spice up whatever needs spicing up.

We now have over forty thousand consultants and claim a 97 percent share of the market for in-home and virtual parties in our product category in the United States. The reason for this is our tireless approach to sales and marketing. Patty and I have worked to find alternative venues to increase brand awareness.

As I say every day of my life, if you want to be successful in business, you need to be willing to put yourself out there and do the grind.

This is how our annual sales have grown from $3 million in 2001 to some $350 million today. We've increased sales 29 percent year after year, during the entirety of my time overseeing Pure Romance. That kind of expansion doesn't happen by accident. And it doesn't come easy. Neither does $2 billion in product sales during my first twenty years with the company.

By the way, the same rules of classiness apply to me when I carry the company banner at consultant gatherings and sales training sessions. I've embraced my role as our head coach (a title I prefer over "motivational speaker").

When I started out giving talks to large groups of people and consultants, I had a significant public speaking phobia. I'm the guy who got a D in his public speaking class in college. That's something I had to work through. It was mind over matter in the end. I never forget that the company is a representation of me, an extension of who I am and the way I carry myself. Patty never forgets that, either.

We now ship all our products out of a distribution center in nearby Loveland, Ohio. (I couldn't make up the name, and some days I still laugh when I hear it.) It's all contract manufacturing, utilizing chemists to design, engineer, create, and modify our exceptional product line.

I'm pretty proud of the fact that we successfully pared down a lot of the tacky novelties we were selling when I signed on, like penis cake pans, boob toppers, and ice cube molds in sexy shapes. Those were the types of products that did nothing for our image. We've been on a journey of evolution since the beginning, and this has helped us all grow with the organization.

It helps too that we're old-school, selling products that people touch and feel and sample in person (unless we're talking about a virtual party). People like to pick up merchandise, smell it, squeeze it, and get to know it, because looks can be deceiving. That's the advantage of an in-home party, though in the pandemic age (which we're still in as I write this), it isn't always possible. Until the COVID-19 crisis, less than 10 percent of our company sales were from online parties. Now those events account for around 55 percent of sales.

Once we were firmly established in America, we set our sights on international expansion. So, between 2010 and 2014, we started operations in Canada, Puerto Rico, Australia, and New Zealand. We found there was a need for what we can supply, so global growth made sense.

What gets me out of bed every morning is imparting what I've learned to our independent sales force, teaching them the fundamental skills to thrive while witnessing their struggles, and then watching them overcome them. I've learned that the most important things people bring to the job every day are their attitude and their motivation, which aren't things you can train people in. Our best employees and consultants have always been heavy-duty self-starters.

It's also interesting how you can turn your negatives into assets. The fact that I suffer from dyslexia means that I don't script my talks or have others script them for me in advance. As a result, I speak off the cuff and from my heart and my head rather than from a piece of paper or a teleprompter. I have bullet points to keep me on track, but that's it. This has ultimately helped me to connect with people in a much more genuine, one-on-one, personal way.

I will also share throughout this book how I've learned during my years at Pure Romance that there is a clear right way to do things and a wrong way. One of the right things is taking care of the city that helped you to thrive, which is why we moved our corporate headquarters to downtown Cincinnati in 2014. We also bring as many of our conventions to Cincinnati as we can, to give money back to local businesses and to the area. We commissioned a study from the University of Cincinnati Economics Department, which found that from 2014 to 2018, our conventions brought over $25 million in revenue to the city.

Moreover, we didn't *have to* buy two of our competitors, Slumber Parties (between 2014 and 2015) and Passion Parties (which was poised to go under, in 2016). But it turned out to be the right move.

The idea of the buyouts started in 2014, when some women left Slumber Parties to join Pure Romance. We quickly found that their company wasn't doing so well. The founder reached out to us and asked if we'd be interested in buying them out. The problem Slumber Parties had was one that I see with too many businesses today. You can't just copy what's out there and assume it will work. The Slumber Parties folks thought they could duplicate some of our practices without knowing how it all fit together for the consultant compensation plan. But they didn't have the back end set up correctly, they were not buying smart, and inventory was a big issue.

We finally worked out a deal to acquire Slumber Parties. The thing is, we weren't really buying its assets but essentially the consultant sales force. It was a little bit scary until we figured out how we could give the consultants a better system. We were successful in helping them basically triple their business in less than two years.

The challenge for us was really in blending two very different companies and cultures. As soon as we figured out how to do it, in came another call the following year, asking if we might be interested in acquiring Passion Parties. Now here was a third company—or as I like to say, family—we were obliged to consider trying to blend with.

One of the owners of Passion Parties had just passed away, and the other asked if I'd be willing to meet at the company's headquarters in San

Francisco. I almost walked away from the negotiating table—in fact, I *did* walk away. But then I saw all of these women who had worked so hard to build their teams and their communities, and I knew there was no other company who could come in and make this deal happen.

I returned to the table twenty-four hours later and decided to acquire the company after all. We absorbed its consultants because it was the right thing to do.

Would it have been easier to let Passion Parties dissolve and just disappear? Absolutely, considering we now had to implement this third family into our company. But in hindsight, I'm glad we went through with it. The new ideas and new way of doing things that those consultants brought to our Pure Romance culture ultimately made our company stronger.

As the Slumber Parties and Passion Parties sales forces learned once they joined up with us, their customers don't buy products from Pure Romance but from *them*.

This is honestly why we've been so successful. We instill a belief in the individual business owners, training them to believe that it's on them to sell and market their products, generate repeat business, cultivate loyal and repeat party hostesses, and build a personal brand they are proud of. Having self-confidence in sales is key, because people don't buy products; they buy people. It's a truth I will be coming back to in this book again and again.

The reason why I sleep so well at night (and by "well," I mean for five hours) is that my focus is on helping people achieve their dreams. Nothing is more fulfilling than that.

## Takeaways

- The best ideas don't need to be your ideas. As long as you make something better, it doesn't matter where the idea came from.
- Progress over perfection. You need to make something as good as possible, but not so good that you micromanage it to death. That's where madness lies. You have to keep moving forward with ideas,

with creations, with your career. Don't let the obsession with flaw-lessness bog you down in details and keep you paralyzed.

- There is a level of risk involved in all growth. Embrace it; don't shrink from it. And don't fear change. Whatever you have, refine it and make it better. Remember that confidence is key. In nearly every case, the most confident person wins, whether we're talking about services, products, or positioning.

# CHAPTER 3

# It All Started with a Talk Show

To help you get to know my mother better, I thought it would be a good idea to present an interview with her. Mind you, I already knew the answers here—at least I thought I did—but I figured that she could tell her personal story better than I could.

**Chris Cicchinelli:** What made you decide to get into the intimacy-product home-party business in the first place?

**Patty Brisben:** Well, it was early October 1983. I had just given birth to your sister, Lauren, my youngest of four children. I was home on maternity leave, and I was craving a little adult conversation over the top of all the "Mommy! Mommy! Mommy!" in the house. So, I turned on the TV to our Oprah of the eighties, Phil Donahue. He had this subject matter one day that just sort of grabbed me: women who were repping for a company selling marital aids.

**CC:** Marital aids being what intimacy products were called at the time.

**PB:** Exactly. And the stories of these women stuck with me. It wasn't about the marital aids per se. It wasn't about the lubricants. It was about how their lives had changed and how they were changing the lives of others, no longer having to live paycheck to paycheck. They were actually enjoying themselves for the first time.

**CC:** Why did that connect with you at the time?

**PB:** As you know, I was working for four pediatricians, making $4.25 an hour, just getting by, trapped in a marriage that left me bored to tears. I wanted better things for my life. More than anything, I wanted quality time with my family, and I wasn't getting any of that.

**CC:** So, there you are, having watched *Phil Donahue*. Then what?

**PB:** The next day, I got a call from Nancy, one of the mothers who I shared carpool duties with. I just bombarded her with questions: "Oh my God, did you catch *Donahue*? Did you hear what they were saying?" And she was pretty silent as I rambled on and on and on about "It's too bad that would never happen in our neck of the woods." That's when Nancy said to me, "I went to one of those parties last night."

**CC:** That had to freak you out.

**PB:** Of course. Nancy was the type of woman you wouldn't ever imagine could even say the word "sex." But she goes, "Yeah, I went with my next-door neighbor." One of her relatives in Dayton had just started her own business, and she said the house was just packed with people. And I said, "But nobody bought anything, right, Nance?" And she says, "Oh my God, Patty. Women were lined up out the door to buy stuff."

**CC:** Now you're intrigued.

**PB:** You bet I was. Nancy finally said, "Patty, I'm not going to tell you what I purchased. But this morning when Frank [her husband] woke up, he looked at me and said, 'That was better than any honeymoon I could ever have imagined.'" So, I asked her for a number to contact the people at F.U.N. Parties. I called up and spoke to a very well-versed consultant, who told me over and over how her life had changed. I decided to take a risk. I ordered the business starter kit and immediately wondered, "What the hell did I just do?"

**CC:** Now you have these bedroom toys and lubricants arriving at our house.

**PB:** Right. And I was worried about what the UPS driver would think of me. I couldn't even make eye contact with him when the box arrived. Here I am, a mother with three young children as well as an infant, and I decide that I'm going to have a party with these products at our house.

I started calling my friends to invite them, and they thought I was crazy but still wanted to come. My husband coached Little League. I was involved with the PTA. We were well known and respected in our community. People like us just didn't do this stuff.

**CC:** What did my stepdad, Bob, think of all of this?

**PB:** I just told him, "By the way, next Thursday you're going to take the kids and do something with them, because I'm having a party at the house. It's the first step in owning my own business." He asked, "What's this business all about?" I told him, and he announced, "No wife of mine is going to sell this stuff!" I replied to him, "Too bad. I'm doing it."

**CC:** And how did that first party go?

**PB:** I was supposed to have fifteen people. But that quickly turned into thirty, then forty. Everybody brought somebody. The giddiness of the women in the room, their excitement, the laughter, it was just glorious. I think I made $500 during that first party, plus I booked five more parties. It all just felt enormously empowering. Everyone left that first party with this sense of camaraderie, that they finally had the right to make decisions on what happened in their bedroom. They didn't feel embarrassed anymore.

**CC:** Now you're into it. What was your next move?

**PB:** As soon as the party was over, I filled a notebook with questions that were asked and comments made, including testimonials the women made about particular products. I was determined to make my parties more than just a fun diversion but educational, too. For instance, if we were talking about lubricants, I would break the category down to discuss what might be a daily lubricant, which would be a more playful lube, and give a reasoning why they were great for you.

**CC:** Why were those details important to you?

**PB:** I thought it was a good idea to incorporate research and give statistics. Women were hungry for knowledge and, more than anything, permission. I was fortunate to successfully tap into their psyche. That was where I worked.

**CC:** Were you comfortable giving descriptions of the products from the get-go?

**PB:** I was definitely nervous at first. In the beginning, I would say, "Okay, this is a lubricant that's heated. Let me show you. If you rub it, does it feel a little bit warm to you? Okay, now take it and use your bedroom breath to blow on it. Now take your finger and taste it." It was about making women feel comfortable with the purchase.

**CC:** How tough was it to keep your day job while doing this and raising us at the same time?

**PB:** It was very hard. I was exhausted all the time. But I was determined. I sat you guys down early on and said, "This is going to be the hardest year we've ever had. I have to continue working at the pediatric office during the day, and I'm going to do my parties at night, but I promise you the outcome of this will make it all worth it. And I'm doing this because I love all of you and I want a better life for us."

**CC:** But you were doing well enough to quit the pediatrician's office after a year?

**PB:** Yep. I'd saved enough from my first year to put a down payment on a house. It also helped that I had five good friends who would consistently host my parties, and then the word spread and their friends would be the next ones to reach out. Interestingly, none of them ever entered the business—something they say they regret, looking back.

**CC:** How long did you wind up working for F.U.N. Parties?

**PB:** From 1983 to '93. The owner, Freddie Wellman, was running things, but she made some major mistakes and her business finally fell apart. She bought a huge building, got sick, didn't have the right people in place—which is always when your company goes down the tubes.

**CC:** This is when you made the decision to go off on your own and start your own company.

**PB:** I didn't have any choice. I had recruited all these people and had a team of people who were demanding and needing product that was on back order. So, I broke off with a couple of other lead consultants in Louisiana, along with my sister, your aunt. I set up shop in the basement of our house and turned it into a product warehouse. We started with fifty-five people total working with us.

**CC:** Yes, I remember that. And you were basically able to turn this thing into a million-dollar company.

**PB:** That's right. But it took a lot of work. Then I put you through a fancy little college, and you got the job with the publicly-traded company and were getting ready to start a job with a tile company in 2000 when you asked to go through my financials.

**CC:** Wait. I thought it was *you* who asked *me* to look at your financials.

**PB:** No, it was the other way around, and then you said, "Holy crap, you've got a million-dollar company here." Then I said, "Wow, Chris, did you think that your college was accepting Monopoly money?" But when you asked to go through my books, I thought, well, I might as well use your college-educated advice, right?

**CC:** I told you I would give you three weeks. Little did I know it would turn into decades. But back then, I just wanted a little time to think about it first, right? Then I heard a radio spot looking for a Guess jeans model, I saw the people flock to it, and I realized people would come out to meet *the* Patty Brisben.

**PB:** And then we got to spend our next three years together in a U-Haul. I didn't know that was going to be your answer to growing the business at the time. I remember how you would lie to me about how long we were going to have to be in the car traveling from town to town talking about the business opportunity and trying to bring in new consultants. It would be an eight-hour drive and you'd say, "It's probably about four and a half, maybe five hours."

**CC:** I'd have to work through your extreme reluctance to get you to agree to present your party at every stop. But on some level, you also must have understood that the plan was going to work.

**PB:** I honestly didn't know. Each time we went out on the road, from our first meeting, it felt like I was being saved from myself. I was used to getting my hands dirty, and now I wasn't. Instead, I had to be the person walking into the room and saying, "Hi, I'm Patty Brisben," leaving people wondering, "Who the hell is Patty Brisben?"

**CC:** And my idea was to build you into a brand. I was determined to create "The Patty Brisben Story." You know, single mother of four earning $4.25 an hour with no business experience and no schooling successfully grows her own business. You were the American Dream come to life. You were the Mary Kay of this product line. You were the prototypical person we were looking for. This industry needed a voice, someone to rally behind, and you were it.

**PB:** Yeah well, I know that's how you've always viewed it. I never particularly looked at myself as a breakout success story, just as a working woman who never gave up. I had no idea what it was going to mean to others, but I guess you knew. To this day, when women get excited to come meet me or stand in line for hours to have their picture taken with me, it blows my mind.

**CC:** But surely you can see now why they would view you as an icon.

**PB:** I understand it better because I give our consultants amazing tools and an amazing opportunity. And yes, I did walk the walk.

**CC:** Talk for a minute about the challenges in having to evolve from being this completely independent woman running her own show to suddenly accepting your eldest son as a partner and CEO.

**PB:** Part of it was the mindset of our society. It wasn't about how much I trusted you. It was the chauvinism that lurked around every corner. Back just after you started with me, we'd be on the road in these hotels, and the management would never once address me as "Miss Brisben." They would speak to you, Mr. Cicchinelli, instead, because you were a man and I was a woman. I think you learned very quickly that this didn't sit well with me.

**CC:** Yes, I did.

**PB:** And if you didn't set the record straight, things would not go forward, because I wasn't going to be disrespected by you, by them, or by anyone else.

**CC:** Yes, I learned that, too.

**PB:** It was also important that you knew my money was my money and I had earned it. I feel like that really helped you to understand women more as you made your way through this business.

**CC:** Not only do I get all of that, but I'd also like it acknowledged that I often came to your defense whenever you were disrespected, one time in particular involving the Queen City Club. May I take a moment to recount that story?

**PB:** Please feel free.

**CC:** Well, the Queen City Club is this exclusive professional business club here in Cincinnati populated by bankers, attorneys, businessmen, and businesswomen of every stripe—the white-collar elite. Someone wrote a letter nominating me for membership, and it was an easy situation. I said, "You know, my mom is always coming there for meetings and lunches. I'd like her to be nominated." So I get a call from a very influential person in town, who tells me, "There's going to be a board meeting, and your mom isn't going to get accepted for nomination or membership."

**PB:** Yep, I remember this well.

**CC:** And I asked the guy, "Why?" He said, "There's this big benefactor to the club who maintains your mom is going to be pushing smut here," that we ran a brothel, all of this other crap. I responded, "Do they understand that I'm already in the club, and I'm the CEO of the same company?" I reminded him that this was a club that for years refused to allow women admittance.

So, I called the president of the Queen City Club Board that morning and said, "I've heard there is going to be a board meeting today at three o'clock. I'd like you to deliver the following message at the meeting: If Patty isn't voted into this club, here is what I will do. I will issue a press release to CNN, Fox, MSNBC, CBS, ABC, NBC, all of them. I'm going to tell them there is all of this stuff going down in Cincinnati: executives denying a woman admittance to a sexist club, glass ceiling, all of it. And I will pay for programming to discuss it on radio and TV.

"And here is what else: I'm going to turn this club into South Detroit. I'm going to get every freaking homeless person who is unemployed and pay them to stand out in front of the Queen City Club, living in tents, with water bottles and rags to wipe your windows when you pull into the lot. Everyone will know that a respected area businesswoman was prevented from becoming a member. Every member will know it. Every woman business owner in the community will know it. Deliver that message and see if they think I'm screwing around.

"Oh, and by the way, I'll make sure everyone knows that half this club's members have our company on autoship every month for her products. I'll expect your answer back later today."

**PB:** That worked out pretty well, as I recall.

**CC:** Yes, you were approved by the end of that day. I'll admit I was a little rough in how I delivered the message. In hindsight, I could probably have said it more tactfully. But I felt I needed to make sure you weren't denied entry into the club due to the kind of products you sold and for being a woman. And I was standing up for you. In my mind, it was also about making sure there wasn't a bully being rewarded for pushing people around—and instead treating everyone equally and with respect.

**PB:** Fortunately, I got some good advice right from the start of my business. It was strongly suggested that I keep my nose clean and my morals up and high while working in this industry. I always had a rule never to sleep with anyone I did business with, ever. Many of the others didn't have the same rule, and to my mind they paid dearly for it.

**CC:** What other lessons did you come away with from your early years?

**PB:** I made sure to ignore the negative voices that told me what I was doing wasn't apropos or proper. I committed to my business and didn't let the opinions of others sway me, ever. Instead, I focused on the outcome of what I wanted for me and my family.

**CC:** Looking back, what do you think ultimately made you so successful?

**PB:** I was always able to stay in the top five in sales and sponsoring even with you four kids at home because I became a student of the business. I literally studied it to understand what it was that women were looking for and why the ladies loved my parties so much.

**CC:** Why do you think they loved your parties more than they did those of some of the other consultants?

**PB:** Mine were different because I incorporated the health aspect of everything, which I think built relationships and trust inside my company. Most of the party planners out there were just about, "Hi. This is water and I drink it. I hope that you'll drink it, too." That kind of thing. Instead, they should tell you everything they can about what water can do for your body, what effect it has, the number of ways you can use this particular bottle of water. I was about making sure that if you were sitting in the audience at my party, you would find a reason to want this product for yourself.

Remember the show *Sex and the City*? Every woman watching it could identify with one of those ladies. Were they Charlotte? Were they Miranda? Were they Samantha? Were they Carrie? That's what I wanted at my parties when I was explaining the products. I wanted every woman in that room to identify with that bottle of lubricant. I was never just describing a product. I was telling a story.

**CC:** You were also creating a very safe environment for women to explore this part of their lives.

**PB:** Exactly right. They could shop. They could ask questions. Then they could go into a private area with me for a one-on-one consultation in a nonthreatening atmosphere.

**CC:** But you acknowledge that my marketing plan for you highlighted by radio and personal appearances ultimately paid off?

**PB:** After you joined, I have to give you credit, we became smart in our marketing. You remember the conservative late-night radio host Bill Cunningham from WLW-AM 700? He called himself "The Voice of the Common Man," his hometown is Cincinnati, and his people would call up to have me on all the time—especially during ratings sweeps periods.

**CC:** Everyone wound up knowing your business from those appearances with Cunningham. It helped you to build more and more traction. But the reason Cunningham liked you is because you were so interesting and entertaining on the air, so articulate and fun. This wasn't charity. You were good for him, too.

**PB:** Cunningham would also always have me on his show around Valentine's Day. That went a long way toward establishing our credibility nationally and in growing the business.

**CC:** Even while growing up with you, I wasn't always aware of how tough it was trying to live and run this business in such a conservative community. I've already told the story about the kid at the bus stop teasing me when I was in middle school. And I remember that certain kids weren't allowed to have sleepovers at our house.

**PB:** It bothered me much more when it impacted you kids, less so when it fell on me personally. I tried very hard to turn a blind eye to all of that crap, because if I focused on all the negativity, I never would have had the energy to move forward. I saw the bias against us, and it always made me angry. But it also motivated me.

There was another instance where the president of the YWCA said of me, "That'll never happen. We can't nominate her for a Career Woman of Achievement Award. We don't want that kind of person." Then they brought in new blood and they changed their tune to "Patty deserves this." I hear the story over and over: "We really had to fight for you, Patty." I'm thinking, "Why should you have to fight for me over something so natural?" I'm helping people's relationships. That's it.

**CC:** The ignorant ones out there have a knee-jerk reaction that what Pure Romance does must be somehow indecent.

**PB:** But of course, the truth is, we're developing products that also help physicians and their patients, like dilators and lubricants. But I will never show that what someone thinks bothers me. Not anymore. I will never again give people that satisfaction.

**CC:** Did you ever imagine that I'd be working with you for more than twenty years?

**PB:** Absolutely not. It's still shocking to me that my passion has become your passion. And vice versa.

**CC:** The truth is that you laid the groundwork for showing women that this was a great business opportunity even before I got here. What I did was pull you away from packing boxes and shipping orders and having to micromanage every element of the business. And you also overcame the men who screwed you over and ignored the people who said you'd never be successful in a male-dominated industry.

**PB:** My focus from the start was making sure women had a voice when there previously was no voice for them. My mission was to provide a safe environment in helping women create their own business. I never cared about having a big, beautiful home and a luxury car. I think most successful entrepreneurs will tell you their motivation was never the trappings of success. In my case, it was to convince women to dig deep and follow their dream.

**CC:** I remember there was a time when many of the products in the various lines would have nasty names and pictures of naked women, as if it were misogynistic men who made all the buying decisions for them.

**PB:** It was just insane. Men were developing these products and didn't have the first clue what they were selling and who they were selling to. They would copy someone else's idea and try to peddle the merchandise with boobs and butts on the box. No woman wants to see that. This is why when I started, I would often put things in a plastic bag with a header card over it that would just give the name and block out a lot of the tacky visuals.

The women I was looking to sell to didn't look like the women who were on those boxes, for one thing. And no woman wants to receive a product and feel like they can never measure up to what's inside. I made it my business to talk to every person in the industry who understood what made their products tick, and I used that information to inform my own products and customer base. That's where I got my college degree.

**CC:** It's interesting. You'd imagine the two of us would think alike and rarely clash. Yet we butted heads a lot and still do, to some degree. My theory is that you were always completely sure of what you did, so you insisted on doing things your way. Meanwhile, I was just as certain of what would work and what would not.

**PB:** We just have different ways of doing things.

**CC:** I agree. But I would argue that our disagreements were rarely about proving who was right and who was wrong. It was about bettering the business and pushing it forward. I think there was an acknowledgement that I could never bring what you do to the table, and you could never bring what I do. The yin, the yang.

**PB:** Let's face it, our issues are also about the fact that I'm a woman who doesn't sugarcoat. I'm direct, to the point, and often painfully blunt. I'm not very good at patting you on the back. I'm not one of those touchy-feely people who will say, "Well now, look at what you did today. How amazing is that?" No. Not me. But if I'm working on a project with you directly, I'll be open and honest. I'm going to say, "I love this, I love this, I love this, but I really think *this* needs to change."

**CC:** You aren't shy about expressing your opinion, I'll give you that.

**PB:** No, I'm not. And I think you and I are a lot alike in many ways. My tone can be off-putting at times. I can speak my mind and then you can say, "When you said this, it made me feel discounted." Just as there are times when I'm so passionate about something and you'll say, "That's really stupid. I don't know why you feel that way." We've each gotten much better, when we're sitting at a table with fifteen other people, at saying, "I don't know where you're going with this, but I think we need to have an offline conversation about it."

**CC:** That's all fine, as long as you acknowledge that I've been good for business over the past twenty-plus years. I think you probably sold $7 million worth of product between '93 and when I joined in 2000. We've sold more than $2 billion worth since I got here twenty years ago.

**PB:** Yes. You haven't screwed things up too badly.

**CC:** I'm also very lucky that I have such an understanding wife in Jessica. She's just been incredible through all of my travel in raising our kids and being so supportive of everything I do as I evolved in the business.

**PB:** That's so totally true. Jessica has been a wonderful partner for you in every way, and the best daughter-in-law. How many ideas do you think you run past her in a given week?

**CC:** Oh, she hears them all, and she has great perspective and thoughts on developing them. She also provides me the honest opinion I need, now more than ever. Definitely my better half.

**PB:** You got that right.

**CC:** But in terms of you and me, I laugh when people say, "Wow, it's so nice that your mom handed you the business." And I'm like, "Are you f-ing kidding me? That isn't the way it's been at all." I feel like we've been true partners, in part because you wouldn't have it any other way.

**PB:** I think it's worked out very well. I could never have envisioned we would grow to be a worldwide leader in the industry.

**CC:** When you meet people and they find out who you are, how different is the reaction you get today versus the one you might have received thirty years ago?

**PB:** Thirty years ago, there was a lot more ignorance out there in terms of what we do. Some still hear "Pure Romance" and think we're a matchmaking company, like fixing people up. Then when I take them on the journey, they'll share with me, "Oh my God, you have that Coochy product, right? I love that stuff." That's our bestseller, as you know—our shave cream.

**CC:** Yep. Anyway, Patty, I think that's all I need for now. Thank you for sitting down with me for my book. And thanks for handing the business over to me. 😌

**PB:** Wait a minute. Did hell just freeze over without my knowledge?

**CC:** (Laughs.)

## Takeaways

- You need to be working both *on* your business and *in* your business at the same time. As tough as it may be, you need to set some time aside where you're working on the bigger picture beyond the day-to-day, because you can't scale and grow your business if you don't put some of your focus on expansion at the same time you're running it. For instance, in the case of my business, I'm currently working with futurists on branding. Never stop thinking about innovating.

- Find your differentiator. Find what sets you apart from other companies, from other businesses. Use that information to widen your footprint and broaden your impact. Your uniqueness will ultimately fuel your success.

- Guard your integrity with your life. It will carry you to the next level, and every succeeding level. Ultimately, all you can stand on is your word.

- When you're working with a relative—in my case, my mother— alcohol helps. A glass of wine never hurt anyone. But seriously, if you want to learn true patience, go into business with your family or close friends. The truth is that when you're working with them, you need to create boundaries to protect those relationships.

# CHAPTER 4

# Be Proactive, Not Reactive

In his classic book *The 7 Habits of Highly Effective People*, which was originally published over thirty years ago, Stephen Covey laid out the seven habits that he believed lead to a fulfilling and successful life. The first of those is straightforward: be proactive. It sounds simple, but in fact it's anything but. It takes focus, will, trust, risk, and confidence, and the absence of any of those will leave you gun-shy.

"Be proactive, not reactive" is a fairly modest concept when you break it down to its essence. It's something many guys learned back in Little League: play the ball, don't let it play you. It's tied to taking the initiative and controlling the narrative.

Proactive people take the bull by the horns and guide it. They accept responsibility for their circumstances and their decisions and go to great lengths to improve and evolve. They don't sit back and let their situation dictate their reality, and they refuse to allow conditions to drive their decisions. They use their values and their common sense to create new choices, and they don't duplicate what everyone else is doing simply because it's the road most traveled.

They don't take the easy way out. They act rather than react.

There are far too many people just waiting for good things to happen instead of going out there and making their goals a reality. It's easy to be reactive, but taking matters into your own hands and being proactive take practice and will.

A simple way to be proactive in your business is to develop your marketing plan. Marketing creates enthusiasm. Start small by reaching out to past contacts and build from there. Sending a personalized text message to fifteen past clients is one way to get people excited about your business.

If you're proactive, you understand that it's about both the journey *and* the destination. My best days all happened while I was on the journey—the hard times when I'd cry myself to sleep, constantly checking my bank account, wondering how I was going to make it. Even though they were stressful, riddled with anxiety, and made me nuts, those times molded me into the person I am today. They are what built up my values and taught me to have an appreciation for the good times I enjoy now.

At the same time, it's not all just about the grinding trek. The destination is equally fulfilling, even if much of the original challenge has been removed. You create new challenges along the way.

Trust me that you're going to experience problems of one sort or another in every area of endeavor. As I'm always telling our consultants, your job is to have different problems next year than you had this year. You want to upgrade them. For instance, in the beginning I was worried about my U-Haul breaking down because my schedule was so tight. Today, I may be worried that because my mechanic is sick, my private jet is grounded. I'm supposed to hit three cities and I'll be inconveniencing a huge number of people in addition to myself by having to cancel.

I say this because I think a lot of people presume that if you have enough money, all your problems magically disappear. Not so. Money just creates a new set of problems. It doesn't make all of the other concerns vanish.

You want to know what being proactive looks like in my life? Until I was grounded in the spring of 2020 by the COVID-19 pandemic, I was traveling more than two hundred days a year for nineteen years. That's roughly four thousand days on the road in just short of two decades. All that travel was about providing constant training and support to manage a remote workforce of thousands of women consultants.

Did I really have to work that hard and travel that much? No. But I felt that if I wasn't out there, I was being lazy. Slowing down simply was and is not in my character. To me, it beat counting on hope to grow my business. Hope alone has never worked for me, just as it hasn't worked for highly successful people like Sara Blakely and Gary Vaynerchuk ("Gary Vee"). They're both realists, and they know you can't simply *hope* that your business is going to get bigger, better, stronger.

This is why when people ask me how I've done it, I'm not afraid to tell them, if they're really looking for my advice, "Look, you're going to work your butt off." Nobody likes my mantra, but it goes like this: you can sleep when you're dead.

As I am also fond of saying, quit looking for the easy way out. Stop searching for the easy shortcuts. They don't exist. I've spoken to a lot of CEOs and really successful people. Not a single one said, "You know what? It was so simple. I've made it to the top of the mountain. Now I can finally relax."

It just doesn't work that way. You know why? Because when you look off into the distance, there's a mountain that's higher than the one you're on. If you're proactive, you have to scale it. There is no "relax" in the vocabulary of successful people.

Most people, I find, don't have a clear understanding of what they want out of life. They tell me, "I'll be honest, Chris. I just want to be happy in my business."

I'll counter with, "Oh really? Tell me what that looks like. How do you measure happiness?"

They'll respond, "I don't know. I just wake up and want to feel good."

"Oh yeah? What does 'feel good' look like?"

"Well, I can get out of bed," they'll say.

"Okay," I'll continue, "can you get out of bed on a bad day?"

"Yeah."

All right, so now we have determined that happiness means being able to get out of bed even when they feel like crap. But just being able to get out of bed doesn't really help fuel a proactive life. Their answer doesn't tell me if they have measurable goals, much less if they're progressing toward them.

One of the ways in which I find that people too often are reactive rather than proactive is in launching their career. They're paralyzed by uncertainty and fear.

When I originally got to Pure Romance, I thought I needed to get that MBA before I could ever think about running a company as president or CEO. Instead, I was just tossed into the mix, because I wrongly assumed that I was just the sum of my education and work experience. That move taught me that you shouldn't wait to get to know everything before taking the plunge.

I've worked with a lot of new consultants who have said to me, "Gosh, you know what? I'll get started when I know more about the products I'm selling." I tell them, "No. Book your first party now. Get up and go now, because the more you think about that first party, the more scared you're going to get, the more intimidated you're going to feel, and the more gun-shy you'll be."

Once you get into that mindset, you're going to overthink it and not invite anybody. You'll freeze with indecision. You'll wind up immobilized, exhausted, and ultimately steeped in failure. The people who procrastinate, who sit back and think about getting every last piece just right before moving forward, don't progress. They get stuck in neutral or first gear and stay there. You can't wait to act until you know everything, because the truth is, you're *never* going to know everything.

Proactive. Proactive. Proactive.

As the world (and in particular the U.S.) continues to evolve, one way Patty and I stay proactive is to look to new markets. That's something we did in 2019 when we rolled out our RGB Collection. In this case, RGB stands for "Red, Green, Blue" (the colors of the rainbow), and the products and toys this collection features were designed to move beyond straight women and heterosexual couples to serve all genders, identities, and orientations.

The embracing of new growth areas continues in 2021 with our introduction of a men's product line. Our goal is to properly serve gay as well as heterosexual men who want to experience our products but might not have the opportunity to attend a party. The goal is to install a male service component online.

This objective of greater inclusion coincides with changes not merely in society but in this CEO as well. I'm continuing to understand and educate myself in the LGBTQI (that's lesbian, gay, bisexual, transgender, queer, and intersex) community. My mother had wanted to go in this direction for quite some time, and I was the stumbling block. But as I've made myself more aware, the move toward inclusion has proven a natural one.

The progression in our thinking at Pure Romance is also evident in the terminology we collectively use. Before, it would be, "Oh, this is for your husband; this is for your wife; this is for your girlfriend, your boyfriend." Now, we are very gender neutral when we talk about a significant other or partner. All of our training materials over the past six years or so have completely evolved.

We'll continue going forward to be inclusive of everyone's sexuality and intimate life, and to make sure that we offer products to help with that. And as far as our parties are concerned—either in-home or virtual— lesbian and trans women are welcomed with open arms. If you identify as female, we want you there.

But there is also admittedly a much more personal reason why I've been inspired to put my focus here. It's LC Marie, my daughter.

LC's assigned gender at birth was male. From the age of three, LC would insist, "I'm a girl, Mommy. I'm a girl, Daddy." I would contend, "No, no, no. You're a boy." But LC didn't want to hear it. LC knew what was deep inside.

Finally, around age eight, the summer before third grade, there arrived a night when LC didn't want to go out to dinner because of having nothing to wear. Nothing to wear in this case meant no girl clothes.

"Okay then!" I remember saying. "We're going to Macy's, you'll get girl clothes, and you'll wear them to dinner." I thought this would prove so traumatic that it would be the end of the conversation. Man, was I wrong.

We drove to Macy's, walked LC into the girls' clothing department, and told LC to pick out anything in the department and I would buy it. LC took a blue skirt and a white top into a dressing room. A few minutes later, LC came out twirling and had the biggest smile.

"Daddy," LC said excitedly, "what do you think?"

"You look beautiful," I replied.

I paid for the clothes. That was the moment when I finally understood that this wasn't just a phase. Suddenly, this angry and sullen young person was a talkative and joyous—and reborn—trans girl. She was leading the conversation at the dinner table that night. It was magnificent.

Still, the family didn't really use pronouns a lot at that point, as my wife, Jessica, recalls: "We wanted to give her an out, just in case. But we didn't need it. LC instantly thrived. During that third-grade school year, she adjusted beautifully, had lots of friends, sleepovers. It was a turning point for all of us on this journey."

Jess got that right. She also remembers what inspired our support for what LC ultimately was. My wife had the *Today* show on in the background and she was half-listening when they began to discuss gender dysphoria among young people. It hit her like a ton of bricks that this was what our child had.

"They started talking about how there is at least a forty percent suicide rate among these children," Jessica recalls, "and you may remember my saying to you, 'Chris, we can't lose our child. I don't know what I would do.' I was determined to do everything to make sure my child was happy and comfortable and confident in who she is."

Our support for our daughter has also gone beyond accepting and advocating for who she is. We committed to becoming change agents in this arena. In January 2018, we cofounded Living With Change, a 501(c)(3) nonprofit dedicated to supporting transgender youth and their families by providing education, resources, advocacy, and support while fostering confidence and acceptance through change.

We forged a partnership with Cincinnati Children's Hospital Medical Center to establish the Living With Change Center for Gender Health, which enhances resources for lesbian, gay, bisexual, and transgender youth and their families. Living With Change began with a $2 million pledge over five years (later increased with a matching endowment for up to an additional $1 million). When my wife and I leave this planet, half of everything we own will go to this nonprofit.

Not only are we helping transgender young people adjust with their families, and in school, by establishing safe workspaces and by promoting policies that ensure their equal access to safe schools, public spaces, and health care; we're also dedicated to turning around the thinking of parents like the one I was. I was initially afraid to enter the transgender clinic and face the reality of my daughter's situation.

As I sat outside the hospital, I wondered, "What am I doing here?" I still didn't want to believe it. I was split fifty-fifty on walking in. I'm glad I did.

My wife, I might add, was down for this from the start. She was much wiser than I was, thankfully. I had to let go of my firstborn son and focus instead on LC's happiness. But I've fully evolved, and I'm proud to call Living With Change a key element of my life's purpose, helping to drive the conversation of educating the public on transgender youth.

Today, my daughter is a happy, healthy thirteen-year-old girl who plays volleyball for her middle school team, takes voice lessons, and hangs out with her friends. She is also right now making some decisions about potentially taking hormones, something she is finally old enough to consider.

"We're just thrilled things are turning out so well for our daughter," my wife adds. "She has had a few issues with schoolmates here and there. The biggest thing is educating people, because they're scared of what they don't know. That's where we hope Living With Change can make a difference."

Coincidentally, our biggest success from a company perspective also happens to be in transforming attitudes. It was my time on the football field that taught me just how important being proactive really is in the business world.

When I started at Pure Romance in the early 2000s, people still didn't treat us like a real business. They would say, "Oh, it's sex toys. It's like *Hustler*. It's like *Penthouse*. It's like *Playboy*." What few seemed to understand was that it was actually about teaching women how to own and operate their own business. The products were always changing, and people didn't comprehend that they encompassed far more than bedroom toys. But those are what got the sizzle.

All of these different groups in our backyard in Cincinnati looked at us the same way. But the treatment wasn't due to malevolence; it was simple ignorance. So, Patty understood that we needed to provide education to evolve the thinking. It was up to us, not them, to turn around the mentality. To be proactive.

Patty has always told me, "You can't fix stupid." The only thing we can do is go out there and make sure people understand that what we do is valuable. And education has been our primary weapon.

All of our fellow intimacy product companies at the time were essentially discount department stores—you know, bringing in and selling everybody's brand at a lower cost. But that wasn't our game plan. We weren't going to peddle videos and anything that wasn't classy. There seemed to be a hole in that market waiting to be filled for the consumer.

Patty wanted to appeal to the customer looking for a high-quality, high-class product, not a cheap knockoff. She wanted to target middle-class women looking to shop slightly above their means. She targeted those who were shopping at Nordstrom or Saks Fifth Avenue, who aspired to buy Givenchy or Gucci. You walk into those stores and you know they've curated the best of the best.

Today, it's also brands like lululemon athletica (athletic apparel) that try to hit the sweet spot of the upwardly mobile consumer. Patty looked to have us offer that superior indulgence one notch up from the middle. That's where we wanted to play.

The desire to provide affordable luxury probably goes back to my grandfather. Grandpa didn't have a lot of money, but he still bought nice cars. That was the one thing he would do, because he prized durability. He bought something that was a little bit over his pay grade, but he knew it would last and that it was a great product. He also didn't spend anything he didn't have. He'd feel really good about that purchase, that it would stand behind him.

We demanded that kind of quality in what we were doing as well. And trust me, this was a revolutionary concept fifteen to eighteen years ago. When I got to Pure Romance, you would walk into a trade show and the buyers all would be men. They would be purchasing for all these adult bookstores populated exclusively by men. That's why you would see naked boobs and butts all over the packaging. The men who bought the stuff for their partners somehow thought, "That's going to turn her on, I'll buy that," whereas Patty and our product team will tell you nothing could have been further from the truth.

The easy way would have been for us to just stick with what was already there. For the longest time, women were not even in the conversation when it came to sex toys. There was just a bunch of guys sitting around a table thinking about what women would want in terms of intimacy products. Patty also understood that women weren't looking to buy vibrators and lotions from creepy guys in porn shops, which they would never enter in the first place.

My mother was determined to curate around women, and it turned out that women didn't really want any of the tacky stuff. That was all for the men. They were looking for something more sophisticated, which was a genuine risk to try to fulfill.

There was a lot of pushback. But we were determined to stay the course and make it happen. It turned out to be the right move, and we're still taking those calculated risks today. I feel like we've ridden the crest of #MeToo and the female empowerment movement by creating products and jobs that take women's refinement and sexual health into account.

In fact, our strategy simply made good business sense. Just like Procter & Gamble understands and plays to the fact that 70 percent of retail purchases are made by women, while 85 percent are either made by or influenced by them.

*Consultant Spotlight:*
## Melanie Frances Allen

*(Lives in: Okinawa, Japan—due to husband's service in the U.S. Marine Corps; six years with Pure Romance)*

"I absolutely love meeting new women and helping them enrich the relationship they have with both themselves and their partner. I've often been told that after attending one of my parties, couples reconnect and build a stronger bond that ultimately saved their marriage.

"My favorite online party theme has been 'Tiger Queen,' a play on the TV show that aired at the beginning of quarantine in 2020. It helps keep things fun, fresh, and exciting.

"My Pure Romance business helped me pay for many infertility treatments over a two-year span, as well as take vacations as a family to Hawaii, Tokyo, Hong Kong, and a cruise of the Caribbean. We no longer stress over my husband's military paycheck affording us the extra, fun things in life.

"I'm looking forward to purchasing a new SUV in the spring when we move back to America while still being able to put at least $2,000 monthly into savings.

"Working with Pure Romance has made me realize that sexual health and understanding the necessity of certain products are key factors to successful sales. The training and information given to consultants in classes provide us with the ability to explain and promote safe, fun, and quality products for all our clients' needs."

Patty basically came in and brought a female voice to an industry that had none, and single-handedly transformed it. When talking about bedroom devices, she asked questions no man would think to ask: "Is this too much power? Is it hitting the right area? What about pulsation? What about acceleration?" And the packaging would describe it in detail.

This approach was mind-blowing, because no one really wants to discuss their sex life, and certainly not in such an explicit fashion. Just recently, I was on a plane talking with a fifty-five-year-old woman who ended up telling me she had never used a sex toy.

Education remains a significant hurdle, of course. Everything that has been built around this business involves a form of social risk. Those who think everybody is evolved and cool with sex toys are wrong. I still have buddies who ask me, "I don't understand. Why would she need this? She's got me."

That's certainly how it was back around the time I started with the company. Having a group of women gather in a home saying, "We're all going to be talking about sex toys" absolutely offended and threatened a lot of their partners. At best, the guys thought it was amusing. At worst, it put a strain on their relationship and became an issue in the bedroom.

It's still controversial to some extent today when we say it's important for women to own and understand their bodies and how they find and experience pleasure. Experts agree that while you can still have a great connection and a rewarding physical bond, achieving maximum pleasure and the utmost intimacy often requires a little help. Research shows that women need a more varied stimulation menu than men to achieve optimal satisfaction.

When I got here, this business was working to change a culture, to alter conservative viewpoints. We had to impart to people who were buying and selling the products that they didn't have dirty minds for being involved with them, that they were normal. There were no celebrities posting to Instagram about this stuff back then, so we needed to convince women consultants that this was a perfectly acceptable way for them to take care of their families, earn extra money, and help stem the divorce rate.

To our mind, thinking proactively, it wasn't enough merely to change the package the products came in and the quality of the people doing the selling. We were also determined to put more academic validation and muscle behind what we were saying.

The research provided to us by Professors Herbenick and Reece at Indiana University helped determine that women who buy and sell our products have better sex lives, take care of their kids, and have good marriages. It normalized our message that a lot of people successfully and seamlessly incorporate what we do into their lovemaking and their relationships.

Yet those who are impactfully proactive don't merely follow trends and fill niches. They also visualize and innovate, and are careful not to emulate what everyone else is doing.

It was Warren Buffett who came up with the idea of "the three I's." First come the innovators, who see opportunities that others don't. Then come the imitators, who duplicate what the innovators have done. And then come the idiots, whose greed undoes the very innovations they are trying to use to get rich. I'm not trying to be an imitator or an idiot. I'm not looking to take someone's idea and knock it off, and neither should you.

What I'm determined to do is get out in front of the next product advancement. That means I need to take more risks and be willing to possibly fail in order to have a chance to be part of the groundswell.

In the case of Pure Romance, this approach is about taking the next bold step in creating an ecosystem for your bedroom, for your relationship, for your communication, and for your sexuality. That's what we at the company need to focus on over the next five years, and it involves not just product modernization but distribution methodology. We already got a taste of how quickly and effectively our consultants could pivot during the early spread of the COVID-19 pandemic.

As a CEO, I understand that nothing that can grow my business is off the table. If you rule out anything based on your taste or ideology, it's a death sentence. You have to be open and willing to change. Staying static is stagnation. Think about Diebold, which for well over a hundred years was in the business of making safes and locksmithing. But as the need for safes dwindled, it shifted gears and got into making ATMs and electronic voting machines in the eighties and nineties.

You want to be Diebold. You don't want to be Borders, a bookstore chain that went under in 2011 because it couldn't effectively evolve with the times and got swept up in the Amazon tornado. You don't want to be Blockbuster, which at one time had more than fifty-eight thousand video rental stores in the United States and another twenty-five thousand around the world. As of this writing, it has precisely *one* store left: in Bend, Oregon.

You have to be open to anything, and when something great presents itself, you need to pounce. Maybe it's virtual reality (VR). If the data says it's right, and the analytics are speaking to you, you must be ready. In today's world, the retail arena around the globe is changing faster than ever before.

In terms of VR, I can't tell you what it will be or when it will happen, but I can foresee virtual reality becoming a part of the Pure Romance product line by 2025 or 2030. Possibly earlier. Experimentation is ongoing.

Holographic technology that allows you to experience things with other people in a different location as if they were in the same room may be the next wave. Think about it this way: if you could figure out a way to take a two-gallon bottle of laundry detergent and shrink it into something paper-thin and save a bundle on shipping and transporting it, that would be a game-changer.

If you aren't in the lab and investing in your future, you're toast. Everything is in play. The Pony Express once thought it was safe. So did Borders. So did a lot of great companies that no longer exist.

Consider this: 88 percent of companies that were in the Fortune 500 in 1960 are either greatly reduced today or have gone out of business. That's nearly nine out of ten. Twenty years from now, there will be commonplace things that we can't even conceive of today. Everything in business is about the willingness and ability to adapt.

You always want to be in front of the change, never behind it. Play to be revolutionary, never ordinary. The worst that can happen is that you may have to go back to the drawing board.

Let's talk for a minute about your goals. I'm all in favor of them. It's important to have something to shoot for. But at the same time, having goals isn't the same as possessing the ability to visualize as part of your proactive toolkit. It's in clarity where power resides. Long-term visualization is what is essential. On the clarity staircase, goals are steps.

The only problem with goals is that you're sometimes going to miss hitting them, and you don't want that to get in the way of your overarching vision for yourself. The best thing about a goal is that it's just something written on a piece of paper. You can rip it up and start over with a new goal.

Our company didn't have a good first quarter in 2019. We were off in our projections by 17 percent. That's quite a bit. But it didn't destroy us. Most people would have thrown in the towel and lamented, "Oh my God, what are we doing wrong?" But having a longer-term vision permitted us to not panic, to make smarter business decisions, and to resist dictating our future based on a single unmet projection.

This mindset is also a corollary to keeping your ego in check. News flash: making a lot of money is *not* about actually having or spending the money. It's about personal recognition. It's about validation. It's about security. It's about feeling you're something special.

Here is something that I see in my company all the time: someone will be at $150,000 in sales for the year and standing as the number-two representative behind someone who did $160,000. That second-place consultant will, on the last day of the year, deposit $15,000 in their account just to beat the other person. They'll take it out of their savings and put it in their sales account, living on peanut butter sandwiches and ramen noodles and wearing older clothes, because it's all about getting the accolades—buying recognition instead of earning it.

Don't let this be you!

We too often allow status to dictate our mindset, our reality. Instead, of course, it's the satisfaction of a job well done—of trying our absolute best and living with the result—that should determine how we feel about ourselves, not some materialistic symbol of success. The problem with such shallow thinking is that nothing is ever going to feel like enough, and as a result you'll always come away unfulfilled.

Having money or recognition as your highest purpose is counterproductive to happiness. Been there, done that. Oh, I love having nice things as much as the next person, but it doesn't set me forward on my path. It can, in fact, have the opposite effect.

This reminds me of the worst piece of advice I ever received: play golf. Forever. As in, retire, sit on my butt, play golf, and relax.

First of all, while I like to play golf, I don't like it *that* much. I play it enough, maybe twenty rounds a year in a good year. I think the guy was trying to tell me, "You're rich. Kick back, enjoy life; you've earned it." But if I did that, I would just be sitting around being bored to tears. It isn't what motivates me. I'm not doing all that I do to generate endless free time.

On the opposite end of that spectrum, a guy I respect a lot once told me, "I'm going to give you one piece of advice in business: be the last person at the table. Don't fold. Don't show your cards. Stay in the game as long as you possibly can, because everybody will give up eventually. Either they can't take the pressure or can't handle the uncertainty."

That suggestion has stayed with me. Can you outlast the pain and the doubt to thrive while you're in the middle of doing a deal? It became my maxim. It can become yours, too.

You know who else was always the last one at the table? The late Kobe Bryant. We can learn a lot from the five pillars of his Mamba Mentality, which are:

1. **Be Passionate.** We at Pure Romance are passionate about our cause and our mission. If you aren't, people will walk all over you. When negativity seeps into your space, conquer it by educating rather than by getting upset.

2. **Be Obsessive.** In business, you must be obsessed with going more in depth and up to the next level of clientele that you wouldn't typically market to. It's about innovation and building your brand.

3. **Be Relentless.** Never give up. It's an axiom that means everything. Too many of us grow too comfortable talking to a particular group, which hinders our branching out. Take the risk and network outside the box.

4. **Be Resilient.** Life will throw you curveballs, and many of them happen when you least expect it (COVID-19!). Always stand firm in the face of hardship and roll with the many punches.

5. **Be Fearless.** Step outside your comfort zone. Fear and trepi-
dation defeat more people than any other single element. They
leave you beaten before you ever take that first step. Push past
the anxiety.

The chief difference that I see between successful people and unsuc-
cessful ones is having a proactive daily routine that inspires them to stay
in the area where they're being most productive, that fuels their consistent
output. It sounds like such a simple thing, but in truth it isn't. Too many
other things get in the way of a clear "What are you trying to work for?".

What should be particularly exciting for all of you women reading
this book is that things have changed so much for the better over the
past decade. We understand today that being groped in an elevator and
treated like a piece of meat are *not* okay—that, in fact, groping is assault.
Women are now empowered to speak out and defend themselves against
predators. They are silent no longer.

Does this mean that, as a CEO, I have to communicate differently
with women than I would with men? I would hope I wouldn't have to.
I wouldn't want my daughters to have to be dealt with differently. You
know, "Oh, you can't talk to Susie and Betty like that, but it's okay to
speak to Steven and Bob that way."

Is the implication that women aren't as strong and therefore must
be treated with kid gloves? I'm delivering the same information to both
genders. When you start genderizing things, you view some people as
weaker or different because they purportedly can't handle the truth.

If I have anything to say about it, this idea will become as extinct as
a dinosaur.

There is one last thing I need to do before moving on to the next
chapter: reassure you that bigger is not always necessarily better, no
matter what area of life we're talking about. Specifically, I'm referring
to companies. Consider that I clear more profit than many billion-dollar
firms that work on razor-thin margins. I would rather be a $200 million
company making a 20 percent profit than a $1 billion one making a 1
percent profit.

I know this is Business 101 stuff, but it bears repeating. This is why you're reading my words. I get it, and once you've made it to the last page, you'll get it, too.

You have 1,440 minutes today. What are you going to do with them? Start by being determined to stay proactive and ahead of the curve. Because once you fall behind, it's awfully difficult to catch up.

## Takeaways

- Being proactive means taking a leap of faith without having all of your ducks laid out in a row. It's so easy to procrastinate and convince yourself that you need to know everything there is to know about a job or business before starting the process. The secret to moving past paralysis and progressing is often as simple as just taking that first step. Don't overthink it.

- There is no reward without risk. Going in for a job interview is a risk. Establishing a relationship is a risk. Committing to sell bedroom toys is a risk. Just crossing the street is a risk. Don't be afraid of it. Embrace it. Nothing that can grow your business should be off the table, but anything that can move you to the next level is also risky.

- The reality of life can be so much better than the best-laid plans. For instance, my daughter began living her true self and best life in a way that wasn't possible as her original gender. And I couldn't be happier about her journey and being there with her every step of the way. Let things play out. Don't interrupt the process. Fate can have its own agenda.

# CHAPTER 5

# Only *You* Can Sell You

I like to say that the sales consultants at our company offer millions of women education, entertainment, and empowerment in addition to great products. What too many people in the sales business fail to recognize is that people buy people. People buy stories. People buy *you*. How you present your knowledge of your products when trying to make the sale is at least as important as the quality of the goods being sold—because at every step of the sales journey, what you're really selling is yourself.

And as the title of this chapter makes clear, no one can sell you but you. You need to deliver a marketing plan with you at the center.

Trust me, as CEO, this applies to me, too. I'm out there selling myself every day, in every way. How do I dress? How is my tone? How's my posture? Do I seem confident? Truthful? Trustworthy? Am I connecting like I should? Am I giving off the proper vibe?

As a guy who was branded "slow" as a kid, who struggled with an undiagnosed reading disability until I was nearly through high school, who couldn't master public speaking until I was well along in my career, I still have a checklist to make sure I'm not falling back into bad habits. The line between fumbling and sprinting across the goal line is often surprisingly thin.

If you're in any sort of business where sales are paramount, you aren't just an order taker. You won't simply be relaying numbers to the corporate office and shipping the goods. There are pre-buys of inventory, sales presentations, and one-on-one meetings with your customer where you forge a relationship. Sales is about nothing if not relationships, connections, and making an impression that lasts.

But more than anything, at the end of the day, it's about how you come across. There are no accidents. It takes constant work, something you probably already knew.

Too often, we fixate and obsess on what others think of us. Your level of success depends on your ability to spend less time pleasing everyone and blaming the world for your failures and more on understanding "If it's meant to be, it's up to me."

Your job here is really twofold: to make "yes" the logical and emotional choice, and to paint yourself as the person they want to do business with. That means presenting the necessary positive image to achieve those two interdependent goals.

Here are thirteen tips for making sure you're selling customers the best possible version of you:

## 1. It isn't about having money but showcasing that you have value.

When I started my business life, I knew that one day I'd be a millionaire. I just didn't know when. I also understood that if I acted like I was making $50,000 a year, everyone would treat me like I was making $50,000 a year. You need to carry yourself like you're money whether you have it or not. If you play your cards right, this behavior will become self-fulfilling.

It gets back to the simple fact that we generally are treated the way we demand to be treated. You dress the part. You act the part. Try this experiment sometime: go into a coffee shop dressed in a tank top, shorts, and flip-flops. Then, the next day, go into the same joint wearing business casual clothes. I guarantee you you'll get ten times the service in the business casual attire that you did in the tank and shorts. It's just human nature to treat people who project quality with quality.

At the same time, if selling yourself matters to you, you don't sell your soul to make a buck. You practice style, grace, ethics, morals, and the Golden Rule. (And I'm not talking about the idea that "He who has the gold makes the rule." That's another topic for another time.) Always keep your dealings on the up-and-up. I know that sounds corny, but trust me that the surest way to fail is to cut corners and do things that would upset you were someone to do them to you.

That said, keep your eye on accruing wealth, which is more important than building riches. Riches are what you have when you win the lottery. You can race to acquire riches and make a lot of money in a short period of time, but you can also go broke really quickly. I want you to be wealthy because you've built a stable business. I also want you to be mentally and physically healthy and thriving in all areas of your life, including your relationships.

## 2. If you believe your business has merit, it will show in how you represent it.

I can't tell you the number of times I've had to endure whispers from people claiming Pure Romance wasn't a real business. It bothered me a lot. It was a battle waged as much internally, in my own head, as it was in my community and the larger world.

Society wasn't going to change. My attitude had to. And it did. Once that happened, *everything* changed.

The other thing to remember is that nothing changes people's minds more than money. When you start making it in volume, that opens eyes. People start to see you as legit. They view your business as real. It's sad, because as I tell people, nothing has changed except their assessment of who you are. It's the sustained revenue growth of Pure Romance that helped us to become agents of change, not what we're selling or our business model. These days, I oversee 186 individual businesses, each worth more than a million dollars.

But it took years for the business community to look at what we do as authentic. That crystalized back in October 2019, when Patty was inducted into the Greater Cincinnati Business Hall of Fame. Let me tell you, considering where my mother and Pure Romance had come from, that was one amazing milestone.

How did it finally happen? Well, we were a $250 million annual business ($350 million now), and we weren't using play money last time I checked.

What percentage of companies in the world get to $250 million? A 2009 *Inc.* magazine story notes, "Research suggests that only one-tenth of 1 percent of companies will ever reach $250 million in annual revenue." That's one in a thousand. Plus, we grew every year for twenty years.

My point is that the attention we finally started receiving—the honors from the business community, laudatory articles in the business press—was no accident. We made it happen by comporting ourselves as if we were worthy of being part of the elite. That's how we saw ourselves, and that was ultimately how others saw us, too. It didn't happen overnight, and it may not for you, either. But if you stay the course, it's possible.

## 3. Stay on an even keel even when you're provoked.

I admit it: I sometimes allow my emotions to get the best of me. Nothing will make that happen quicker than having someone go off on a tangent against CEOs and their compensation. Oh man, does that get my blood boiling. These critics never take into account the sacrifices that some of these executives make. Instead, they just gripe that the execs are earning X amount more than the average employee.

What they fail to understand is that people like me didn't earn much for the first decade while growing the business and that, if you look at my hours versus my salary, I've probably made two dollars an hour. I promised myself that if I ever wrote a book, I would make this point that you shouldn't cast aspersions until you've walked in a CEO's shoes for a day. And if you think it's not a fair system, put in the time and become a CEO yourself.

Another thing that grates is the idea that as the CEO of a direct or multilevel marketing operation, I'm overseeing some sort of pyramid scheme. No! No! These are real women running real businesses. Our consultants do not just take orders and ship the products out to their customers. They are in charge of the marketing. They're selling. They control inventory. They figure out their own payroll.

Here is how I tell those same consultants to respond to the pyramid scheme charge: every business—not just traditional multilevel marketing operations—is, in that context, a pyramid scheme. You have a CEO at the top, vice presidents beneath him or her, directors beneath them, then managers, and so on.

I could break down every business in the world and show you that it's in some ways a pyramid. Mark Zuckerberg runs a pyramid of sorts at Facebook. Sara Blakely has one at Spanx. Elon Musk has one at Tesla. Jeff Bezos has one at Amazon. Heck, Amazon is the biggest pyramid setup going. The President of the United States must be running the biggest multilevel marketing program there is.

But don't get me started.

This is a long-winded way of saying that you shouldn't sweat the small stuff. You should let things roll off your back. Don't be like me! (Just kidding. Be like me—in most things, anyway.)

(Pure Romance's legal response as to why we are 100 percent *not* a pyramid scheme is simply this: "Unlike a pyramid scheme, where individuals make money only by recruiting other people, the primary source of our consultants' income is retail sales of products.")

## 4. Embrace "the power of one."

There is a lot of power in the number one. One number, one text message, one phone call, one class, and one customer can change your entire business and life. This concept goes back to focusing on your relationship with your customers. A simple handwritten "thank you" note or genuine interaction with a single person can turn that person into a lifetime customer.

You're selling them by selling you.

Always look at your business as a relationship. You never want it to get stagnant, so it's key to focus on how you present your brand. That means being knowledgeable about your products and excited to teach

*Consultant Spotlight:*
**Kelly Ellis-Neal**
*(Lives in: Fishing Creek, Maryland; eight years with Pure Romance; five years with Slumber Parties; thirteen years total in the business)*

"What I love most about this business is being able to motivate and inspire people to live their best life from the bedroom to the bank account. I go live online at least five times a week and get a chance to network with some amazing people. I feed off the positive vibes.

"Chris Cicchinelli has helped my family to become mortgage-free and save for retirement. No one teaches this to you in business school. He showed me how I could downsize my life, upsize my living, and live life by design rather than default. He also has guided me in how to eliminate clutter from my life.

"When I joined Pure Romance, I had a five-year plan, but within nineteen months I was able to pay down $117,000 of my debt and create a fresh start. Over the past seven years, I've hit every goal I've set and become number one in the world for the company in sponsoring. I now understand how to work smarter, not harder, because opinions don't pay bills—enthusiasm does!

"Since the pandemic, I have managed to completely pivot and turn my business 100 percent virtual. I believe everything happens for a reason, and this crisis has made us stronger and more versatile businesswomen.

"Sexual health matters. Intimacy and pleasure are so important to our relationships. I scream from the rooftop, 'This is what I do for a living!' because if you don't own it, what's the point?"

people what you know. Genuine enthusiasm for your job and the task at hand are infectious.

Use Walt Disney as your model. He was so phenomenal at what he created, and so skilled at selling it, that his customers wanted to see what he put out into the world again and again and told their friends and family. Even decades later, Disney's genius in selling himself and his belief in what he produced leaves people in awe. To this day, his company sells not just a brand but an *experience*.

When you demonstrate the power of one, you change your "I think I can do this" mindset to an "I *need* to do this" imperative and watch your business evolve for the better. Ultimately, selling yourself is like working out. You put in the work, and the results come back. By the same token, if you don't do the grind and put in the time, nothing will happen.

Your decisions ultimately determine your destiny. And you have one opportunity to make your business, and your reputation, shine with each customer. Don't waste it. Just zero in on a single person and interaction (in tandem with your resolute attitude) and magic will happen.

## 5. Be sure to go the extra mile.

Too many business owners sit back and play defense, constantly worried about maximizing profits, competitors infringing on their turf, and so on. But as I've always reminded Patty, "Let's play offense and tell our story before they make one up about us. Let's control the narrative." At the same time, we have been focused on educating people about what we do and surprising them by doing more than was expected.

Case in point: we got involved in our community early on by putting our money where our mouth was. We always contributed as high a percentage of our income as we could. We made sure we got out there every year and gave away more and more money. The first year it may have been $500 to the Susan G. Komen Breast Cancer Foundation. Then it was $5,000 at the Pink Ribbon Luncheon.

We started becoming more and more recognized in the Cincinnati community because of our charitable donations. Then, instead of going to Las Vegas, we started having our annual conference right here in Ohio due to community outreach and economic impact. To our mind, we were selling ourselves as much as we were benefiting and helping to take care of the area.

This kind of effort comes back to treating people with respect and advancing those who share your backyard with you. It also includes helping finance local restaurants and businesses that can benefit from the visitor dollars. The respect for us went up exponentially as we ramped up our area investment.

Does this tell us we live in a particularly materialistic world? Yes. There is a great divide between the haves and the have-nots in terms of the amount of cash you bring to the table. I wish that it weren't that way, but I'm realistic about it. I figure that if I'm a good person and my faith in my community is genuine, good things will come my way as a result. It's turned out to be true.

## 6. Your approach needs to be about expressing gratitude and joy.

Gratitude is the best attitude. To succeed in life and in business and sell yourself to the world, always be grateful for the things you *have* rather than pining for the things you *want*. Your vibe of gratefulness comes through and sells you more winningly than perhaps any other single element of your persona.

One thing I've learned throughout my career is that you can't live in both fear and gratitude at the same time. The two will always butt against each other. Practicing gratitude and allowing that trait to shine through works to reduce your fears by shifting your perspective from fear and uncertainty to optimism and hope. On the other hand, those who don't practice gratitude are generally unhappy, because they're dwelling on things that are out of their control.

Even if you don't have your heart in it at first, strive to shift the negative narrative to one in which you focus on your abundance. When you do, a light will turn on and everyone will be able to see it in your eyes, even if you initially have to fake it a little. Lead with your gifts rather than your sorrows, trepidations, or anxieties.

Part of living a gratitude-focused life is to flood your mind with reflections on your progress. All too often, I see business owners crush a goal and that's it—they just move on to the next thing. Life is significantly more meaningful when you put time aside to celebrate your accomplishments and victories. It enhances your mental stability and makes achieving future goals much more satisfying.

At least equally important is the fact that people who focus on the positive and the good transmit that same sense to their coworkers, their customers, their family, and their friends. You want to do business with those people, because their positive impression leaves you feeling inspired.

## 7. Understand that determination is necessary to build success.

Typically, nothing worth achieving happens overnight. You know it. I know it. Even your dog probably knows it. Getting in shape, whether it be physically, mentally, or financially, takes time. None of us wants that pain, that anxiety, but it's often a necessary step to having a better body, a sounder mind, or a more robust financial life. The thing with this kind of pain is, it subsides over time. It's the short-term sacrifice that brings you the long-term gain.

Conversely, it's easy to read an unmotivated person. They sit back and allow the conversation to control them rather than being assertive and on top of it. I have absolutely no stats on this, but I'm guessing that the more determined you are, the more successful you are. I know one thing: I hate dealing with people who are apathetic or listless in their manner. It shouts to me that they just don't care enough to succeed.

By the same token, I'll admit right here that patience isn't my strongest suit, and for that reason it's something I often work on. It drove me a little crazy that it took me ten years at Pure Romance to officially become a millionaire. I'd always hear, "Well, you're a millionaire on paper," which made me nuts. There's a big difference between having it on paper and having it in your bank account.

For too many people, immediately isn't fast enough. And if something doesn't happen as quickly as they snap their fingers, they lose interest. You don't want to be that person. Instead, you want to be the one who doesn't bail at the first sign of trouble, who stays in for the long haul, who communicates a vibe of patience and determination and brings a sense of stability to the table.

I would rather risk being the one who stays too long at the party than the one who takes off before the action begins. That should be you, too. In essence, don't give up on things. Let them play out. Understand that good things take a while to evolve. It goes hand in hand with your evolution as a person.

## 8. Remember that patience is an essential ingredient in achieving maximum success.

You rarely hear about the months and years of hard work behind the scenes that go into making an iconic brand. Often, businesses need to be brought back from the brink of collapse to ultimately thrive.

Take the case of Federal Express. It was founded in 1971 with $94 million in seed capital but was on the verge of bankruptcy two years later when the founder flew to Las Vegas and played blackjack with his last $5,000, which he turned into $24,000. He was therefore able to keep his payroll going for another few weeks. FedEx turned its first profit in July 1975.

Jeff Bezos ditched a cushy Wall Street gig in 1994 to sell books out of his garage online with a company he named Amazon. He did nothing but lose money for the next several years and was still $791 million in the red in 1999. He didn't turn his first profit until 2003, nine years after founding the company and six years after taking it public.

The sports megabrand ESPN launched in 1978 and soon needed a $1 million cash infusion from Anheuser-Busch to keep it afloat. It didn't turn its first profit until the mid-eighties. Elon Musk incorporated Tesla in 2003 and didn't see his first profitable quarter until 2013, a decade later. Bill Gates founded Microsoft in 1975 and spent the next decade prepping it to go public—in 1986. As recently as 2005, Facebook still faced a yearly net loss of more than $3.6 million. In 1997, Apple was just ninety days from going under entirely.

It bears repeating: nothing happens overnight, or even close to overnight.

By 2020, Apple had a net worth of an astonishing $2 trillion, Amazon more than $1 trillion. Facebook and Microsoft had a market capitalization north of $500 billion, Tesla $450 billion, and FedEx and ESPN $60 billion. It dramatically underscores the point that patience can pay off big. None of them started out like gangbusters.

## 9. Be willing to make sacrifices.

It may surprise a lot of people to hear it now, but when I was growing up, I was one of the poorest kids in my school. That's not a knock at my mother, who did the best she could (and then some). It's just a fact. It stayed with me and still drives me. If you know how it feels to be poor, you never want to feel like that again. This knowledge also helps me in dealing with women business owners who might be struggling themselves.

I literally had no social life in the first years of the business. I was in the middle of nowhere doing trainings while my buddies were at the club, pushing me to come. I've always lived within my means. Plus, when my buddies were urging me, "Hey, we're having a *Monday Night Football* party—come!" or if it was the weekend, I was too busy building the business to join them, even though I definitely wanted to. Erecting a legacy requires sacrifice and commitment.

What I've always believed is that you have to put in the time and effort to achieve anything great. You have to be willing to give up the short-term fun for the longer-term security.

People's misperception of me can be a little frustrating, because I know how hard I've worked to get where I am. The funny thing is, the success of Pure Romance has bred in people the false impression that I was fortunate to have chosen a product category that everybody was into, that sold itself—which is so untrue. We had to change social behavior to get where we are. I had to eat a lot of crap along the way from business owners who thought we were somehow beneath them.

But the reward ultimately has come, and that's what you need to see as an aspiring salesperson. Your prize awaits you for your hard work. A lot of the people I knew way back when don't have the financial flexibility today that I do. I have choice and the ability to do what I desire, which I think is the most valuable currency we have today. Even more so than money.

So, don't be afraid to give up something now for a payoff down the road. People will see that and respect you for it, and they'll want to have a hand in your achievement.

## 10. Stay focused on your goal and your routine.

Every woman has a reason for getting involved as a sales consultant with our company. It could be running from a bad job or a bad marriage. It could be simply not having enough money. It may be credit card debt. Not everyone wants to tell me their reason, because it's often deemed too personal. Money seems to be the most forbidden topic, one that people just don't want to bring up, even more so than sex.

One woman who *did* tell me her reason was Christine, who had $60,000 in credit card debt after ignoring her payments for five years. (It happens that 87 percent of households in the U.S. have debt, and the average household credit card debt is $5,700.) She had just obviously overspent in relation to her income, had completely ignored the bills, and now was paying the price.

Christine started a really strict plan to pay down the debt by slicing her spending to the bone. She personally gave me her credit cards and was able to knock off $18,000 the first year. She called me in tears—happy tears, I assumed at first.

"I can't do this anymore!" she complained to me.

"What do you mean?" I asked. "You paid down almost a third of your debt in a year. You're ahead of schedule on the five-year plan. Keep up the good work! What's the problem?"

"The problem is, it's not happening fast enough."

"Well, hold on," I replied. "Tell me again how long it took you to build up the $60,000?"

"Five years," Christine admitted.

"Well, what makes you think you should be able to take down in one year what it took you five years to accrue?"

"I just want to make it happen," she reasoned.

I think she wound up paying off the debt in two and a half years, which is precisely half of five. Accomplishing goals is all about just putting yourself in a routine and making it happen. In this case, her goal was to get completely out of debt. Anything that moved her toward that, even if she was taking baby steps, was progress.

This is what you need to remember: stay focused on the big picture and be true to yourself, and that will sell you. No one expects you to be perfect. We get ourselves into debt, drink too much, get traffic citations, and screw up right and left. But if you're moving constantly toward improvement, no one will begrudge you your shortcomings.

## 11. Embrace change.

How do you handle sudden business change? Do you sulk and whine, or do you embrace the shift and use it as momentum to propel you forward? As a business leader, I know that learning to pivot at any moment is fundamental. If we at Pure Romance learned nothing else from the COVID-19 crisis, it is that having the capacity to quickly recalibrate, turn, and develop a new strategic direction is key to our success.

People have a natural aversion to change. Why? Because the unknown is scary. Unexpected changes can make you second-guess your decisions, stalling the business you worked so hard to establish. Change leads to growth. When things aren't going the way you anticipated, reevaluate and make adjustments where needed so you can keep pushing your business beyond all limits.

Consider the example of Starbucks. The coffee giant started out as a company that sold high-end coffee beans and espresso equipment. When founder Howard Schultz recognized the need for a coffee shop that could serve as a gathering spot for Seattle residents, he switched things up and started selling coffee by the cup instead, taking his business to the next level and meeting every change along the way with confidence and fortitude.

Remember that while certainty is never certain, you *can* be prepared to modify the narrative. When you're controlled and self-assured in embracing sudden change, you're thinking outside the box and expanding your footprint. Be mindful of the need for change and look for it as a way to rejuvenate your business. Also, keep an eye out for the silver lining in every situation and be adaptable.

The people who succeed aren't necessarily the ones who always get it right the first time but those who master the art of the pivot. That can be you, too. And the ones who are best at pivoting invariably sell themselves most successfully.

## 12. Turn rejection into a positive.

Negative responses inevitably are going to come your way, often even when you think you've done a great job at something. This shouldn't throw you off your game. The next time you find yourself stressing about your business, take a minute to ask yourself, "What is the worst thing that someone could say to me about my business, and how would I react to hearing it?"

Once you have a solid response strategy in mind, you'll be prepared, and nothing can take you down. You'll already have thought through a worst-case scenario, and you'll be ready to handle it.

We all have a tendency to overcomplicate things, whether it be life or business issues. My theory is that we do this owing to a natural fear of rejection. When someone tells you they don't want to do business with you, or they reject your product, or they aren't sure if your business is the right fit for them, it can feel like they're rejecting the core of your very being—*if* you allow it to.

In reality, the worst thing that can happen is not being *prepared* for rejection. One positive and practical way to overcome any objections is to sit down in advance, write them out, and work through possible responses. Preparation, you see, is the key to seamlessly running your business.

Being ready for these doubts, complaints, and rejections and having your response ducks in a row, as it were, is likely to keep you focused, hopeful, and motivated. It will give you the confidence boost that will assure you nothing that comes your way can throw you off your game. It also will drive down any potential stress that may come between you and your selling of yourself.

## 13. Productivity is the name of your game.

Productivity and success go hand in hand. That's no news flash. Productivity is really about three things: eliminating distractions, creating a motivational playlist, and getting organized. I know, it's easier said than done. But becoming more productive is surprisingly simple once you've mastered the art.

First, turn off your phone notifications. Getting rid of that particular distraction will help you focus and complete your tasks faster. Second, create a music playlist to motivate you while you work. Studies show that 90 percent of business leaders perform better while listening to music. Then get organized with lists and whatever else you need to stay on task. Being organized boosts productivity, saves time, and eliminates stress.

Here is another tip. You know those tasks you just dread, like making cold calls and reaching out to past customers whose interest has faded? Perform those first thing in the morning. When you get them out of the way early, you'll suffer much less anxiety during the rest of your day.

The bottom line with this stuff is that a productive person is someone everyone can recognize as a leader, a go-getter, and a success. That's the type of person we all want to be in business with. We want to be their customer because we innately believe they will take care of us. They'll have our back. By contrast, the person who comes across as absent-minded instills a sense of chaos rather than trust.

Start with something simple, like taking a chore that you promised yourself you would do later and getting it done now instead. Be the person who feels like they're controlling their day rather than being controlled by it. That's how you become more productive, and how you demonstrate you have your act together. It's how you have a successful business.

Always remember to dress for the part you want, not the part you have. And at the end of the day, believing is achieving, and achieving is believing.

## Takeaways

- Customer personalization is key, because we're daily being reviewed more than we've ever been. You have to remember that not every customer is the same. Every interaction is unique, and you're going to have to individualize and personalize more than you ever have before. How the transaction goes down makes all the difference in whether you have a one-time sale or a customer for life.

- We get instant assessments these days on Yelp, Glassdoor, and others, and it can be both a blessing and a curse. But in the age of social media, it's something we will all have to live with going forward.

- People buy people, not products. I have a relationship with a certain car salesman whom I've bought from for a long time. I could probably get it cheaper if I went somewhere else, but I wouldn't get the same care and experience as I do with this guy. The guy looks at my value as a longtime customer and doesn't just try to sell me new cars, but also looks at the maintenance record. He doesn't just make me feel good walking out of there after that one purchase. He follows up with me to make sure I have everything I need as a vehicle owner and sends on new car news and updates when they come in. He follows my company in the press and knows things about my family. He makes it a point to reach out and stay current in my mind. He takes care of me. I think I've bought fifteen cars from this salesman, and that's why.

- You are the trusted resource. The relationship you have with your clients should go beyond business. You need to be the expert on your relationship, on knowing details about the person you're doing business with. But it also has to go beyond business. It's important to know more about them because you're trying to create customers for life. Learn their hobbies, their lifestyle, and who they are as people, and the benefits will come back to you in spades.

## CHAPTER 6

# Commit to the Process, Detach from the Outcome

We live in an impatient world. How many times have you sent an email to someone and found yourself irritated when, ten seconds later, they still haven't responded? Or God forbid it should take more than fifteen seconds for a text to be sent due to a poor Wi-Fi connection.

That email has probably been routed all the way around the world and bounced off a satellite out in space at least once in a miracle of modern technology, yet it frustrated you to the point of outrage that it took an extra few seconds for it be seen. Our expectations have grown increasingly ridiculous.

This is how crazy our impatience has become: if we learn that something is going to take a bit longer than our stamina will tolerate, we're liable to throw up our hands and give up on it. If the result isn't immediate, it isn't worth it. The self-defeating sense of exasperation is one of the primary sources of failure in the rapid-fire business world.

This gets back to the fact that we focus almost exclusively on how long it's going to take to get to the end result rather than on the value of the process required to achieve it. Nobody is playing the long game anymore. Everybody wants instant gratification, instant feedback on how well they're doing. Yet when you're building a business—building anything really—you're not going to get a rapid response. It simply isn't part of the deal.

The chief complaint I hear from my Pure Romance consultants is, "My business isn't growing fast enough. I want to crank this thing up." Meanwhile, they can be working not even close to full time and taking in $4,000 a month. Not too shabby. But in their mind, it's all about the outcome. *How* is this going to pay off? *When* is it going to pay off?

These are the wrong questions to be asking.

I don't care if your business is growing at a rate of 100 percent a year. People will ask, "How come I'm not growing at two hundred percent?" This is a consistent refrain that I hear today, and part of the problem is that everyone is obsessively looking at Facebook, at Instagram, and at Twitter, and they're comparing their business and their lifestyle to those of thousands of others on social media. Making these kinds of comparisons exponentially increases the stress about where they should be in their lives and what they need to be earning. It sets the entitlement bar sky-high.

I've had many of these same issues myself. I'm putting in all of this work. Where is my money? But it's the wrong approach, because it discounts the process and skips to the outcome—which never works. Instead, you plant, you plant, you plant, you sell, and then ultimately you reap that harvest. It's a procedure that can never be rushed.

This is why I've based an entire chapter on the concept of committing to the process and detaching from the outcome. It's that important in the scheme of ramping up and sustaining your business as an aspiring owner-entrepreneur.

I like to share these four steps in training someone to look at the journey rather that the destination:

1. **Focus on doing it right, not quickly.** There is a technique for almost everything. If you take the time to do things correctly, chances are you'll get to the result you want faster. That goes for dieting, exercise, business—almost anything. Think about

how many relationships go wrong because people don't take the time to get to know each other well enough before they move in together or get married. Or think about how much more recklessly and dangerously you drive when you're in a rush, to shave maybe two minutes off your trip. What was true before remains true: haste makes waste.

2. **Train your eye on doing it better.** In football, I learned that once I got the technique right, the sky was the limit in terms of how much I could improve my performance. Minus the technique, I'd have been inconsistent and likely have wound up suffering an injury. I knew when playing football in school and now in business that anything worth doing is worth doing well.

3. **Practice patience.** And yes, as I can assure you, doing things slowly does take practice. The sense that something will take longer than expected leaves us frustrated, despondent, angry, and annoyed. We look at people with successful businesses and want what they have, but somehow we don't feel it necessary to put in the years of hard work and sacrifice required to get there. Some of it is the entitlement culture that too many young people are growing up in today. The practice of patience, by contrast, isn't about complacency or laziness or a lack of passion. It's about having the staying power to ride out the hard or boring times and keep chasing a goal.

4. **Celebrate milestones.** This may sound minor on its face, but it's actually tremendously important. The first time you make a sale, celebrate it. The first time you get a big order, celebrate it. Think of it like building a house. The end goal is living in that new home when it's beautifully furnished and decorated, but there are dozens of smaller achievements to rejoice in along the way.

As an adult, you understand that your life can't be all about play and no work if you want to achieve something meaningful. For instance, I hate the treadmill. It brings me little in the way of joy. It's drudgery. I have to force myself to stick with it and see my exercise regimen to the end. But I hit that treadmill every single day, whether at home or on the road, because I crave that outcome of great physical and mental health.

But I don't focus on that end goal. While I'm running, I zero in on what I'm doing right then and there. Every time, I monitor my heart rate, listen to my breathing, and exult in improving my condition. That's how I not only stay in the moment but convince myself never to skip the workout. I make the process itself interesting, so the final result matters less.

In football, I went out and caught a lot of punts. A *lot* of punts. I caught so many punts that I got great at it. Catching punts became automatic. The same went for practicing shooting free throws for the basketball team. I shot a heck of a lot of free throws, and my success rate ended up being 90 percent. This goes back to fundamentals. You practice, you practice, you practice, and then you practice some more.

On a punt, the ball's in the air. You're tracking, tracking, tracking. Okay, now you're underneath the ball. Your arms gather. The ball's coming down. The process is getting in position to catch the football with maximum efficiency. The outcome is what's going to happen after you catch the ball. The process of shooting a free throw is everything you do to prepare before releasing the ball. The outcome is whether or not it goes in the hoop.

In sports and in business, too many people shortchange the process to rush the outcome. Then they want the sure thing. Unfortunately, that isn't how you travel the road to success if you really want to find a pot of gold at the end of the rainbow.

Look to the example of the beauty pioneer Estée Lauder. By the time she passed away in 2004, at ninety-seven, her eponymous cosmetics company was among the world's biggest. What is less known is that it took twenty-seven years of patiently building for the woman who started the company to make it to the top.

At the age of eighteen, Lauder was selling to hair salons a beauty cream that her uncle had developed in her hometown of Queens, New York. She demonstrated her product on women as they sat under hair dryers and gave out free samples. As her customer base grew, she and her husband would whip up their products in the kitchen of a onetime restaurant.

It was twenty years before Estée Lauder was registered as a corporation, in 1946, and another seven before it launched Youth-Dew, the product that sealed the company's destiny as a leader in the field, in 1953. Along the way, Lauder changed the face of sales in the cosmetics industry, training her workers to touch their customers, apply creams, and perform demonstrations, all common practices at cosmetics counters today.

That's what you call a true commitment to the process. The outcome turned out to be spectacular, because Estée Lauder did it the right way in paying her dues and trusting that success would come when it came.

She wasn't concerned that her ultimate reward might be delayed, because she believed in herself and what she was doing. You know what she didn't worry about? What people thought of her. At least, I'm guessing that's the case, or she couldn't have been as successful as she was.

Unless people are as patient and smart as Lauder, they tend to spend above their means no matter how hard they try not to. They feel like what they earn is never enough. I can pay somebody $100,000 a year, $120,000, $200,000—doesn't matter. It's still not enough for their lifestyle.

I was with the CEO of a nice-size business the other day. I know exactly what he makes, and it's not a small amount. Yet he was struggling to make ends meet. He literally didn't have enough money to live on.

"I don't know why," he told me, "but I'll admit to you: every new little toy and gadget, I've got to have it."

Well, that's his problem right there, of course. Guys like him are living for the moment and not building a retirement account. They're always putting it off for another day. But see, I get it. When I finally became a multimillionaire at age thirty-seven, I went a little crazy. Bought a big house. Bought a Bentley and souped-up BMWs. Picked up some $30,000 watches, just because I could. But I quickly realized that wasn't a viable life path, and stopped.

I also used to be especially concerned about how people viewed me, until I realized it was really none of my business. Now I tell our consultants, "Quit worrying about what people think of you. There are always going to be those in your business and personal lives who are looking to take you down, for whatever reason. Ignore them. They aren't worth your angst."

Why is it that we instinctively care more about what our detractors or the one negative person in the group thinks than about what those who are supportive think? In a room of fifteen people, it becomes all about making the one dissatisfied person happy, when that's probably never going to happen. We ultimately give that naysayer far too much power.

As I tell team leaders, you're never going to please anybody if you concentrate on trying to please everybody. In fact, you're going to be miserable. That's just reality. We focus too much of our attention on the squeaky wheel, on winning people over so we can get their affection, get their love, and get their acceptance. I constantly see that among leaders today, because nobody wants to be unliked.

The fourteen out of fifteen people in that room who are loyal and want to see you succeed may not be the top rainmakers for your business. But what they do have is your back. They're moving forward with you. They have no agenda to drag you down.

My mother was the one who warned me early on, "The people you're going to try to win over and help the most will also be the ones who hurt you the most." Words to live by.

A similar vibe exists in social media and other parts of the online world, where people tend to get rewarded for negativity and threats. It's terrible. I've known people who brag about it. They complain about their hotel room, threaten to give the place a one-star rating on Yelp, and in return receive a bigger or free room. It's really a form of extortion. Businesses will do anything today to avoid a bad review, so they acquiesce.

Also, as a result, whoever makes the most noise controls the narrative. Everyone falls all over themselves to satisfy the disgruntled party. I personally get reviewed, too, on Glassdoor by unidentified former employees. I never know my accuser. Anyone can review the CEO, the hotel, the restaurant, the club, and the hardware store, and remain cowardly anonymous.

*Consultant Spotlight:*
## Ashley Coen

*(Lives in Delaware, Ohio; nine years with Pure Romance)*

"What I love best about being a Pure Romance consultant is that I'm 100 percent responsible for my success or failure in my business. Being in control is truly humbling and liberating.

"When I need to kick up my business a notch, I look for a super fun way to present the products. In today's world, we all need more positivity, humor, and education, and I find Facebook Live to be an instant way to generate conversation and business.

"I have learned to dream because of Pure Romance. I am thriving in my personal life because of this company, and the financial success I've set my family up for is life-changing. Consider this: We will be millionaires by the age of forty, with five rental properties. We also have plans for family vacations every year. We're working toward 200 percent growth this year with our team.

"The pandemic has been a giant blessing in disguise for my business, allowing me to learn and focus on e-commerce while doubling my opportunities to make sales. I utilize social media even more to connect and network, and the numbers don't lie.

"The way we sell intimacy products offers a safe space for women to learn about their bodies, receive permission to explore their sexuality, and generate ideas on how to increase pleasure in their relationships. We're changing the way these items are presented and sold. We take pride in being pioneers for empowering women inside and outside the bedroom."

But what if we all got reviewed for our conduct every day? Suppose we were ranked with stars for our behavior. Can you imagine how personal rankings would change the game? That's where real accountability would come into play.

Earlier in my Pure Romance tenure, it regularly frustrated me that our company wasn't being accepted by the wider business community. I finally had to say to myself, "Well, Chris, ignore the naysayers and earn it. Keep doing what you're doing and quit worrying about the outcome of their respecting you." That ultimately worked for me.

When you commit to the process to the exclusion of the outcome, everything starts to fall into place and makes sense. It was the same when my friend complained to me last week, "My friend unfriended me last week on Facebook."

"Well, then I guess she wasn't really your friend," I offered.

"How do you think I can get her back? Did I do something wrong?"

My question became, "Why would you want this person back?"

I like to listen on Audible to books by Brené Brown because there's no fluff. She's a researcher, and things are pretty much straightforward and black-and-white. There's not a lot of gray area with her. She uses a quote from a speech that President Teddy Roosevelt gave on April 23, 1910, called "The Man in the Arena." It has so much resonance, even more than a century later, because it speaks to getting into the ring and fighting even when we don't know what the outcome is going to be.

Here is the key part of that address:

*It is not the critic who counts; not the man who points out how the strong man stumbles, or where the doer of deeds could have done better. The credit goes to the man who is actually in the arena, whose face is marred by dust and sweat and blood; who strives valiantly; who errs, who comes up short again and again, because there is no effort without error and shortcoming; but who does actually strive to do the deeds; who knows great enthusiasms, great devotions; who spends himself in a worthy cause; who at the best knows in the end the triumph of high achievement, and who at the worst, if he fails, at least fails while daring greatly, so that his place shall never be with those cold and timid souls who neither know victory nor defeat.*

Yes, we business owners must get in there and fight without letup. And no matter how it turns out, we will live to fight another day. I guarantee you that there have been days when you, as a business owner, fought and weren't sure you were going to survive. But it's important to remember that building a successful business is a marathon, not a sprint.

Part of moving forward effectively is having a clear objective. A couple of clear, strong objectives are all you really need. When I got to Pure Romance, my objective was this: How do we get from $1 million to $5 million? First market, grow, and scale the business, then change the packaging. Simple.

Let's take a moment here to talk about money, which I'm guessing is the main reason you feel compelled to absorb this book in the first place. Let me just say that my best years in business are the ones when I don't worry about money, when I just commit to the process and let the result take care of itself.

In short, you need to quit obsessing about being a millionaire. Instead, do the things that a millionaire does. Wake up in the morning, put your armor on, and go to battle, even when you don't know what the outcome is going to be.

You know the thing we're all searching for? The sure thing. And it doesn't exist. Why is that what we're focused on? Because it's the mindset that was instilled in us growing up. We need to be *certain* that we will make money from a venture, *certain* that we will get a paycheck, *certain* that we will earn a salary. But I tell people, "In being an owner of a business or an entrepreneur, or wanting to be wealthy, there is no certainty. There is nobody who is going to tell you, 'If you follow this exact program, there is a 100 percent probability you'll become wealthy.'"

Yet I'm often asked, "Chris, if I work really hard, am I going to make millions of dollars just like you?" All I can answer is, "Look, I can guarantee that if you work your butt off every day, you'll feel good about what you're doing, about making progress, and I promise you'll be happier with your life than you are right now. Those are the only guarantees."

Here is an analogy I like to give in speeches: Imagine that we're all sitting in a room together and we see a big-screen TV on the wall. On the TV screen we see a table, and on this table is $10 million. It's right there in front of us. All that stands between us and that money is a wall. It's a

Credit: *Shadow Woolf*

sure thing. It's 100 percent certain. Every one of us will figure out a way to get through that wall to get to the money.

Now let's take the same situation, except that there's no TV screen showing a table with money. I tell you there's $10 million on the other side of the wall, but you have to take it on faith. All of a sudden, you guys are saying, "Let's break through the wall and get that $10 million!"

But after five hours of struggling to bust through, one person asks, "Man, what if it's not there?" Everyone else assures him, "No, no, it's there. Keep working."

Then maybe two hours after that, somebody else gets tired and says, "Maybe Jane's right. Maybe it's not there." Again, most of the people rally and say, "No, guys, keep going."

Finally, the questioning mindset starts to filter through to everybody else, because nobody can see the money. "I'm working my butt off, what if it's for nothing?" That thought keeps trickling down until everyone gives up because the money is not guaranteed. Is the money there? Probably. But now they'll never know.

If you're committed only to the process, your faith in the end justifying the means will be inherent. And it gets back to the balance question, which is one I get hit with a lot. You can't win the game of quantity, because enough is never enough. You'll burn yourself out. You'll get frustrated by where your life is at and by playing the whole comparison game.

Even if you're working all the time, you're going to see other people doing business from a beach, or a pool, or a ski slope, and you'll get frustrated and wonder, "What am I doing wrong?" I believe we all have life roles to play, but I'm not a big believer in balance per se. I believe in work-life harmony. I have my CEO role, my parent role, my provider role, and my husband role. Sometimes they clash, and I have too many people whom I want to be at the same time.

We all struggle to find the sweet spot and live the lives we think we should be living. This is why when I go into the rooms at our training sessions, I see a big part of my job as teaching our people to be better versions of themselves. That includes inspiring them to gain confidence and assuring them they're worthy of having more.

Confidence will ebb and flow, but that's what I want people to walk away with from every single meeting. They keep coming back because they get that shot of adrenaline that assures them they do deserve success and that success is abundant in the world. It isn't limited to just a few people.

One of the most important things I teach business owners surrounds protecting their self-confidence and their mindset around their business. Success isn't just about being the best possible salesperson. I see a lot of great salespeople who are broke. It involves having the proper mentality around money and overcoming the obstacles.

I see too many people who think it's going to be easy, automatic. They sit back and say, "Gosh, I don't want to do that. That seems way too freaking hard." I'm trying to instill in business owners the notion that they need to learn to do the things that nobody else wants to do, the uncomfortable activities that everyone else shies from. A lot of people want to stay at home and make their fortune from there. I would be bored out of my mind, but they think they'll be able to prop up their feet and the riches will just pour in.

It really gets down to the fact that in business, we all live for those moments of glory. We all want to be in that football situation where it's fourth down and twenty-one yards to go, we fling the ball into the end zone with a Hail Mary pass, and *touchdown*! The crowd goes nuts. Pure Romance consultants all go crazy for that time when they've just had the most successful in-home party ever and everyone is telling them how great they are.

But it's a different story when the cheering stops and we have to motivate ourselves again. Nobody is cheering for you when you have to write the emails, make the phone calls, send the text messages, and do the essential grunt work. We love to get that recognition, but we hate the process that gets us there. And if we hated it a little less—if we made that a goal in itself—we would ultimately be far more fulfilled.

I don't just preach this. I walk the walk.

When I was spending more than two hundred days on the road every year for the better part of two decades, people saw me work hard and put the time in. I believe that ultimately helped influence those who fed off my example in a positive way. We are what we see, what we hear, and the behavior we're around.

Perhaps you've heard that each of us represents the average of the five people we hang out with the most. I like to think that I'm one of the guys that a lot of people put into that sphere and they think, "Man, I'm really able to learn something from this dude." People can hopefully learn from me how to grind it out, how to persevere, and how to put a process in place and detach from the outcome. I want them to watch me and receive a lesson in how to put repetition into their lives.

The key in the sales game is really knowing how to have a conversation, how to talk to people. A consultant, you see, is a creator of an experience, not just a salesperson. Make a connection with people and engage with them; don't simply assume what they need and want.

It's a privilege to think I can instill some of my positive work ethic in others. The thing is, I don't get to see the change overnight. Instead, I'm fortunate to witness their journey, their evolution. That said, one of the hardest things I deal with in a day is getting my mentality into the heads of as many people as possible.

My mantra: be stronger than your strongest excuse.

Let me tell you the story of someone who exemplifies everything I just described. I won't break her confidentiality, but she's twenty-one, one of our new Pure Romance consultants. She has an eight-month-old baby but no boyfriend, husband, or significant other. The father is not in the picture, certainly not in a positive way.

Anyway, every morning she'd pull herself out of bed at six and jump in the shower, and for thirty minutes she would stand under the water and just cry and cry. She'd get out at six-thirty, dry off, get dressed, get her baby ready, drop the infant off at daycare, and hustle to work at her twelve-dollar-an-hour job that she took for the health care coverage.

She'd work there from eight a.m. until five o'clock, pick up the baby, race as fast as she could to her parents' house, drop the baby off, and hold a product party, which she would do three or four nights a week. She'd get done with the parties at eleven o'clock or midnight and either crash on her parents' couch or take the baby home. The baby, meanwhile, had colic and would wake her up two or three times a night.

As all of this was going on, the baby's daddy was sending her messages telling her what a slut she was, how she was this, how she was that. I remember her breaking down and crying on my shoulder, saying, "What am I doing wrong? I feel like I'm such a failure."

This young woman sold $50,000 worth of product in that year working her business. I assured her she was anything but a failure. That, my friends, is committing to the process and detaching from the outcome in spades.

So, when I hear people gripe to me about not having enough money or enough fun or enough support, I tell them about this young lady who denied herself a life to make sure her baby had a better road to travel than she did.

I learned more from this young woman's will than I could have in years of business school. Fortunately, I was able to connect with her in an effective way. As I've learned, communication is the real key in business. Even during the COVID-19 crisis, we were able to do it effectively with our sales force, and it has made all the difference. I teach consultants how to market themselves, what it means to be a brand, what it means to control inventory—I help them understand what they have and how to make and keep themselves profitable.

I also teach, and preach, commitment to the task and detachment from the ultimate result. Put in the requisite energy and focus, and let the rest take care of itself. Doing this is easier said than done, but so is everything. And whether you know it or not, *you* can do this.

## Takeaways

- Whatever game you're playing, you have to play to win. But remember that you're never going to please *anybody* if you concentrate on trying to please *everybody*. More than anything, you have to please yourself.

- It's about effort over excuses. In life and in business, too many people make excuses for why the outcome didn't work. You need to commit to the extra meetings, the extra phone calls, getting out of your comfort zone, and going the extra mile. When you're planning for the next six months, the next year, or the next two years, you need to take a look at where the process can break down, the efforts you need to put forth to stay in the game, and the steps that are integral to progress.

- One thing I've learned over the years is that money can't be your sole focus. I understand that it has to be pretty important or you won't be in business long, but you can't think about money and *only* money as your motivation. My best years in business are the ones when I don't worry about money. That can't be the primary reason you do what you do, or you'll never succeed.

## CHAPTER 7

# Live Your Life by Design, Not Default

Too many people live their lives by default and not by design. While most of those I meet tell me they'd like to have a better job, a bigger house, a nicer car, all of the accoutrements of success, they too often fail to be the architect of the design that would help them procure the things they say they want. They let life live *them* instead of creating their own unique blueprint.

I'll elaborate on what I'm talking about.

How many people do you know who simply do what they think they're *supposed* to do? They attend grade school. They grow up. They graduate from high school. Maybe they sign up for a trade school or a sensible college. They graduate from college. They find a partner and get married. Settle down. Have a kid or two. Buy a Volvo or a minivan. They get the house with the picket fence. And they're done.

Call it a life—right?

Now for a lot of us, this sounds like hell. It's the kind of hell that doesn't allow for us to choose the life we crave. Maybe we want to custom-design our life. The problem is that people don't believe they can do that. They don't understand that they're in charge of this thing. They design a kitchen, they design a bathroom, and they design a bedroom, but they never think about sitting back and asking, "What exactly do I want for my professional career?"

Everything in our lives should be like a buffet. Maybe you want an eight-ounce steak with peppercorn and a little béarnaise sauce on the side. Maybe you want your carrots to be caramelized or glazed. You create the path; you craft your own life buffet. No one else is going to do it for you.

You have the controls. Whether you choose to use them or not is entirely up to you. But you get to do all your own customization. Maybe you want to emulate the way this person interacts with people, or that guy's sales technique, or the way this lady plans events. All of those pieces or people that you're seeing are materials you can incorporate in designing and building a work life to your custom specifications.

You can make things happen and create a new you at any age. It's about having the will to reinvent yourself and establish new goals.

Some people give up before they even start. They're completely paralyzed for a variety of reasons. Maybe you're one of those people. They're so common that I've given them names. You don't want to be any of them if you plan to be a winner.

- **The Procrastinators:** They are always putting off until tomorrow what they can do today. They want things to get better in their lives, but they don't have enough money, enough resources, or enough friends. They'll do it once the kids get a little older, once they retire, once this, once that. They put happiness off into the future. When they were twenty, the goalpost of happiness was *here*. Now, at thirty, it's *there*. It will never be right in front of them. But it isn't just success and contentment that they're pushing off to some unknown date. They're pushing off everything of consequence, from desires to security to travel. "I'll do it when it's convenient." What they want never happens.

- **The Quitters:** They give up. When the going gets tough, they drop out of sight. In their mind, they set the bar so high that what they want to do can never realistically be achieved. It's an impossible ideal. And a lot of it stems from what they see on social media, the idealized lives that people put out there on Facebook, on Instagram. Ninety percent of what they're seeing is an image being buffed by influencers rather than a genuine lifestyle. They sit back and wonder, "How come that guy's doing so little and driving a Bentley? I've been working my butt off and I'm not even remotely going in that direction." The glamorous life they can never attain kills their self-confidence and self-worth, leaving them mired in self-doubt and, finally, self-defeat. More people want to be led than be leaders, and influencers prey too often on the weak.

- **The Self-Criticizers:** Too many women business owners are overly critical of themselves. They seek but get no accolades all day long, so they'll pick out every flaw about themselves and their business, and they'll be nicer to a stranger than to themselves. Not only is this mindset spirit crushing, it makes it extremely difficult for them to design their lives, because they're too mired in misery to move forward. Meanwhile, they pursue validation and love from the people who withhold it from them the most. They need instead to wake up every day and understand they are the only person who can control their bliss.

- **The Self-Limiters:** They think that because their mom or dad made only thirty or forty thousand bucks a year, that's going to be where they should look in terms of their limitations, too. Maybe they moved back in with their parents. They alternate between menial jobs and unemployment, and they think this is as good as it's ever going to get for them. They don't even see a path to independence with their own apartment or house. Education is the way to change that belief and instill some understanding that altering this mindset is not only possible but essential. Change is inevitable, but growth is an option.

- **The Fraidy-Cats:** Yes, I'm using the term "fraidy-cat" in my book, but it's to make a necessary point. These people are afraid to take a chance and risk both success *and* failure. The fear of failure is only part of it. "I'll just keep things the way they are, even though I'm not really happy, because it's too risky to my status quo to try to change," they think. They don't know how to handle success, either. "Oh my God!" they worry. "What if it works out? I'll be so tied up with my job that I'll have no time for myself. No one will ever leave me alone!" These people get too comfortable with their mediocrity, and it's their very comfort with ordinariness that traps them on a treadmill to nowhere.

Do you see yourself in any of these stereotypes? Hopefully not. But it's important to recognize that in order to reach any aspirational goals, you have to create a design that will establish a pathway to get you there. Minus that design, too many distractions or other priorities are bound to get in the way.

Any age or stage is the right age or stage to create your life design. Age is another of those things that people use to hold them back. "I'm too old" or "I'm too young" or "I don't have enough experience."

These are all just excuses.

I was President of Pure Romance before I turned thirty. As I write these words, I'm forty-five and a far different person than I was in my twenties. But I don't regret having designed my life so early. The tweaking of that design continues as I go forward.

Neither youth nor age has stopped some people in the past. Being in your early twenties or late fifties shouldn't hold you back, either. Consider:

- Wolfgang Amadeus Mozart wrote his first symphony at age five.
- Anne Frank was thirteen when she started writing her wartime diary.
- Gymnast Nadia Comăneci was an Olympic champion at fourteen.
- Mark Zuckerberg was nineteen when he launched Facebook.
- Beyoncé was thirty-two when she ranked number one on the *Forbes* Celebrity 100 list, worth $115 million.

- Reporters Bob Woodward and Carl Bernstein were twenty-nine and twenty-eight, respectively, when they exposed the Watergate scandal.

- Sam Walton was forty-four when he opened his first Walmart outlet.

- Ray Kroc was fifty-two when he bought his first McDonald's franchise.

- J. R. R. Tolkien was sixty-two when he published *The Lord of the Rings*.

So you see, you can change the world at any age. It's all about having the courage and the will to reinvent yourself and generate new goals.

When I was a kid, we used to play a game called MASH (not to be confused with the feature film or television comedy set during the Korean War). The letters stand for Mansion, Apartment, Shack, House. It's like a game of life that we learned in the fourth grade. It might involve being married to Jane or Cindy or Betty. How many kids will you have? One? Five? Twelve?

MASH also asks what kind of car you'll be driving. A BMW? VW? Mercedes? Will you live in a mansion? How many rooms? Where will you go to college? What will you major in? How old will you be when you get married? Where will you go on your honeymoon? What kind of pet will you have, and how many? What city will you live in? So many decisions.

You can even play MASH online now, at https://mashplus.com/, or download it as an app. Regardless of how you play, part of the message we can take away from that game is that people usually spend more time planning their next vacation than they do developing and scheduling the kind of life they truly want to live.

We become a reflection of our choices, and I believe there are significant ways of impacting those choices through proper planning. For a very long time now, I've planned for how I want my life to look and play out. I've tried never to get wrapped up in the day-to-day at the exclusion of my larger plan. Too many people quit plotting things

### *Consultant Spotlight:*
### Zara Zay (Part I)

*(Lives in: Ann Arbor, Michigan; twenty-six years in the business)*

"Pure Romance quickly became my primary source of income after just a few short months in the business, when my faith in joining was confirmed by success after success as I journeyed out to conduct in-home parties with our products. I happily turned in my steakhouse server apron and jumped full steam ahead into the new company.

"Beyond skills I have cultivated to stir up laughter, woo an audience, and build countless friendships alongside life-altering financial gain through sponsoring and mentorship, I am proud to offer sexual health and wellness education as a primary focus. In the words of my very successful father, money is just a byproduct of something you do well.

"I love the flexibility of being a Pure Romance consultant, which includes being my own boss and the freedom to work whenever, wherever, and with whomever I choose. The size of the nuclear bomb that goes off in my head when someone tells me what to do is considerable.

"People don't give a hoot about what you are selling until they experience how genuinely you care about their lives and individual needs. The consistent practice of DWYSYWD (doing what you say you will do) and reaching out daily to be of service promoting our Pure Romance products have proven to be an endless golden formula for cooperative excitement.

"I now have my own health coaching practice and dance and yoga studio. I own forty acres of land. I'm assisting paying off a home for my sons. I have more than $100,000 in savings in the bank. None of this would have been close to possible without this company."

out at a certain stage and simply accept the life that's been presented to them.

When it's time to get a job, they get one. When it's time to marry, they do. When they see everyone around them having kids, so do they.

Through the years, I've worked with a large number of people who just go with the flow. They travel where the tide takes them instead of controlling their destiny, pushed in whatever direction the winds happens to be blowing. They are, in short, allowing others to directly or indirectly determine their path, and more than likely they wind up far from their preferred destination.

In my more than two decades at Pure Romance, I've seen a lot of people struggle financially. The recession that hit in 2008 was good for our business—we do much better in a down economy, when there is more desperation and people seek out a side hustle or second job—but bad for the country.

During the COVID-19 crisis and record unemployment, which we're still dealing with as I write this, more people have been struggling than perhaps ever before in my lifetime. To them I say: take action. I so often hear, "I want a better life; I want a better job; I want more time with my family; I need another income stream to take the pressure off." Whatever it is that you want, I'm here to tell you, it's there for the taking.

All you have to do is commit the time to designing a plan to get it.

Let's speak for a moment about how you're going to create a living-by-design game plan. Living by design is one of the valuable lessons I learned from being involved in sports in high school and college. A big part of it is sharing your goals so there is a commitment beyond yourself. Consequently, getting everyone (including your spouse and kids) on board with your plan in advance will go a long way toward staying zeroed in on it.

Make sure you write down your goals. Don't worry about failing. Everyone does. It's what you do to move past the failure that counts. Also, revisit your life design often, as it's a living, evolving thing that will regularly spin into new areas.

One of the people whom I saw turn her life around through successful design is Amy Hoelscher, a consultant who had struggled financially for a long time through several direct sales consulting attempts. When a friend invited her to a Pure Romance party, she was stunned to see a near traffic jam caused by the forty women who showed up.

The friend convinced Amy to become a consultant herself. But after she received her first product kit, she realized she was too uncomfortable to move forward. She tucked it away in her closet, and there it sat for two years.

A series of mishaps worsened Amy's financial life. Her husband was in a serious car accident and couldn't work. Their vehicle was repossessed. A fourth child had just been born, and after they fell behind on their mortgage, they were about to lose their home.

Amy recalls, "My husband and I got in our car and drove around, talking it through. Things were dire. Our house was going to be sold on the courthouse steps in two weeks. We needed a plan. Part of that was my trying Pure Romance parties out for a month to see if it could make a dent in our finances."

She made calls, sent texts, floated an appeal to her friends, retrieved the product kit from the closet, planned parties, and started making money. She had those friends over for her first party, sold an astonishing $6,000 worth of products, and saved her house. She built her business from there. Amy made $18,000 in 2010 and $90,000 in 2011.

In 2014, Amy's team sold $1.4 million worth of product. In 2015, she racked up more than $220,000 in sales by herself. In 2016, she became a Pure Romance executive director. Today, she can boast of having broken $2 million in career personal sales and is now completely debt-free. Considering where she came from, her accomplishments are nothing short of amazing.

"The greatest part is that this doesn't even feel like work to me," Amy says. "It's just a part of who I am. It's helped so many dreams to come true for me. And I know that no matter what happens in my life, I can stand on my own two feet and take care of myself and my family. I'm in control. The kind of self-confidence and sense of self-worth that's given me is priceless."

Amy adds, "Before I started working with Pure Romance, I didn't know intimacy products were a normal thing. But after several parties and hearing from customers, I learned that having toys and accessories doesn't replace anything; it just spices up what's already there. That was huge for me."

Here is another story: Seven years ago, Julie Salter was working as many as sixty hours a week as a produce manager for a Safeway supermarket. She was no longer feeling challenged in the slightest. But she also didn't imagine she deserved anything more. She was, after all, not long out of the South Boise Women's Correctional Center, had only a little bit of college under her belt, and was earning twenty dollars an hour.

"I thought grocery retail was as good as it was going to get for me," Julie recalls.

That was when a friend working in the supermarket's bakery department mentioned something about bedroom toy parties for a company called Passion Parties (then our competitor). "When she told me the commission was forty percent with no glass ceiling on what I could make, I was more than intrigued," Julie says. "I signed right up."

Julie also thought right then and there that she was going to leave her job and run this business. Based on what her friend had pocketed ($500) from her first party, Julie figured she could do two to three parties a week, quit the supermarket, work part time, and earn the same or more than she was taking in while working in produce.

"My second full calendar month in business, my sales were $10,000," Julie says. "Now I earn a six-figure annual salary, and I've moved to Arizona and bought a house with a pool and a convertible while working part-time. Talk about swimming upstream against the odds. I'm running close to a million-dollar business, have no debt, and have over a decade of drug sobriety under my belt.

"When women tell me about their hardships and struggles and situations, I assure them they can always change their stars. They just have to be willing to do it."

This is a good place to remind you that life is *not* a walk-through, as Amy and Julie could assure you. If you're just going through the motions and letting other people make your choices for you, you've given up control of your destiny. Your life is officially in default.

An essential element in shifting your personal and business dynamic is to have real, planned objectives to meet. There are so many demands on our busy lives that make it easy to grow weary of the grind. We get distracted by social media. We become caught up in the naysaying about us or our business. This is why it's necessary to have a road map to keep us focused and avoid getting discouraged.

I like to call this an internal GPS. Using it creates an externalized GPS that becomes action. There will still be roadblocks and construction that will make it difficult to get where you need to go and potentially derail your progress. Sometimes I allow other influences to intrude on my focus, too. But no matter the challenges, just keep moving forward.

It's all about prioritizing. Sometimes, I will take a business event off my calendar to spend more time with family and friends. As a parent, I'm often left believing there's never enough time with my children and, until the pandemic hit, I felt guilty having to be on the road so much. In the end, however, everything I do is for my family—and my wife and hopefully my kids recognize that.

You also need to consider that if it all feels like sacrifice, maybe you need to change up your life, your relationship, or your goals.

Goals aside, there are two things that I believe are critical for everyone to know about themselves: their *why* and their purpose. The *why* question is focused on what gets you out of bed in the morning, what makes you do the work that you do. My wife and children are my *why*. They're my priority and my responsibility. I have a commitment to do everything possible to provide for them. They are my *why*. Pure Romance is my vehicle.

As for my purpose, it's something that will stay with me long after my kids are grown and (hopefully) have become independent adults. Because of how I grew up and saw my mother working so hard as a single woman, I determined early on that I needed to help women—not just help them be successful with their plans for themselves and their families, but empower them to thrive.

The importance of purpose is that it helps you marshal your energy to have a larger impact beyond your current circumstances. It's part of a legacy you'll be remembered for. It may sound a little bit Pollyannaish, but I want to leave the world a better place than I found it, and my work with Pure Romance is part of that. I want my consultants to live better lives by setting goals, being financially independent, and becoming responsible business owners.

I take pride in being an agent of change in my company, which for me means using a microphone and educating people to modify the way they feel about something—such as, say, sexual enhancement products.

Or let's say you have drunk only boxed wine your entire life and know nothing different, and then I serve you a nice bottled cabernet. I could educate you on how it feels when it hits the palate, how it smells, how it tastes, and how it entices you. That kind of instruction is positive, too.

Of course, a lot of people don't want to be educated. They're fine with their limited information and comfort zone, and they grow uptight when you try to introduce something that makes them rethink. This is why, instead of just talking about our products, I want to change beliefs through information, through facts and my own experience—not because I'm right and others are wrong or ignorant.

A lot of what I try to teach in my training sessions is simple common sense. I preach respect for people. Number one on that list is to respect other people's time. If your appointment is at five o'clock, don't show up at 5:05.

Remember that you have to be the responsible one in the room, because it's never a given that the other person is. They may simply be ill-informed, relying on stereotypes and outdated ideas instead of reality.

I'll give you an example. My mother and I always go into meetings in business suits, which surprises some people. They imagined that because of what we sell, we were going to show up in black jeans, a black shirt, a black jacket, a leather skirt, gold chains, the whole guido thing—because, you know, Cicchinelli is an Italian name. Meanwhile, the lawyers we meet are the ones who are dressed casually, because they weren't expecting a professional meeting.

Education clearly can take you only so far, and common sense unfortunately can't be taught.

Another thing that people do is overthink things. Let's say they want to write a book. Instead of getting busy planning it, they'll start a focus group. What should the book be about? Should it be a sales book or something else? Should it borrow ideas from other books? Be entirely original? On and on and on. You wind up thinking the thing to death.

You know what the culprit is? Too much idle time. People ask too many questions. They have too many people in the middle giving them advice. That isn't leadership; it's madness. These same people can't even plan a workout without getting ten opinions. They wind up rescheduling and rescheduling and putting off and putting off. It becomes like a firehose that just explodes.

This is why I live in the mindset of "Let's get it done!" Like Nike says, just do it.

From a "by design, not default" perspective, take it from Tony Robbins. He assures us, "Most people overestimate what they can do in a year and underestimate what they can do in two or three decades." Use your idle time wisely and it will turn into useful time. By the same token, I tell people not to try to make things happen in one 365-day sprint. Spread things out but progress methodically toward your goal. Staying productive is key.

To their credit, our consultants at Pure Romance mostly get it. They are taught to be experts at overcoming negative attitudes and perceptions, far more than someone just selling makeup, and they succeed because they've been empowered to run their own show. As a result, they take ownership. My job is to inspire them to understand, "You've been led your entire life. Now it's time for you to lead."

I tell our women every day, "You're your own CEO." I'm not doing their business. They're in charge of their own marketing, their own inventory, their own everything. People are buying "Pure Romance by Betty," from a personality more than a company. Our consultants sell themselves.

I'm very fortunate to work with an amazing tribe of women who take pride in doing something not everyone could do. None of them went to school to sell sex toys and vibrators, to sell lubricants, but they do it and do it brilliantly.

I have heard too many women in our society say things like, "Well, I don't really deal with the money; my husband handles all that kind of stuff." Drives me nuts. For one thing, I've found that women are generally a hundred times better than men at controlling the family finances when given the opportunity.

When I travel and I'm in a room teaching between two hundred and a thousand women each night, or I'm leading a virtual meeting online, I'm privileged to be able to teach each of those in attendance how to live a better life through financial independence—being responsible for their bills and understanding the mistakes their parents may have made while not getting caught up in that same cycle.

Another thing that motivates women who become business owners is that perhaps for the first time in their lives, they're getting validation for who they are and what they're capable of.

Think about it. Hardly anyone stands up at home and says, "Mom, those pancakes this morning were the best ever!" or, "Wow, my room smells so good, Mom, thanks for cleaning it so well. You're the best!" or, "Honey, you look amazing today. And what a dinner you cooked last night! You're unbelievable."

This happens pretty close to never.

Far more often, women hear, "I'm not hungry for that, Mom" and, "Sweetheart, what have you been doing all day? Why didn't you dust the living room?"

So, when these women have an opportunity to get recognized for their sales savvy, to be honored and praised for their work, they will claw for it. I put a little certificate in front of them and they are nearly in tears.

Why do we need that when we ultimately should be validating ourselves? Why do other people's opinions and endorsements weigh so heavily on our self-respect, our choices, and the things we aspire to? I see this all the time among people working in America.

Doing any of those things would go against my purpose. There are multiple ways I could go out and sell, but none would give women the opportunity to change their lives the way selling through Pure Romance does. I'm pushing to make many women wealthier.

Every one of those people is an important piece of our company brand. I make sure they all understand that each of their moves matters, from the way they treat a bellhop to how they address an in-home party hostess to the way they interact with every customer. It can take a long time to build a brand and seconds to ruin it.

People in business today fail to heed the importance of branding at their peril. This is why you need to look at yourself as a pop star or other celebrity. It doesn't mean you have to be "on" all the time. You just have to do the right thing—and we all know what that is—and you'll never have to worry.

Personal behavior and accountability really lie at the heart of living your life by design. Live it with morals, ethics, integrity, and honesty, and you'll be good. None of us is perfect, but perfection is what we must strive for. Otherwise, we're just living someone else's default.

## Takeaways

- Stop living on autopilot. Snap out of it. You need to step back and ask if you're really living the way you want to live. You need to ask yourself, "What would my life look like if I took the winding road?" You ultimately become a reflection of your choices, and those choices should be uniquely your own, not those of a majority opinion or a collection of influencers.

- You need to be searching for things to change your life and out networking, adding people to your life who can motivate and inspire you. The most effective way to progress and evolve is to find the people who did life right and embrace their ideas.

- Go search out the materials and start putting your life together. If you feel safe and comfortable, you have not reached—and won't ever reach—the level of your true ability. That's when you need to dig deeper, because you're living your life by someone else's rules. You're living by default, with a paint-by-numbers life easel.

*With my mother Patty fronting the Pure Romance Annual World Conference Awards Show in 2018 in Cincinnati.*

*Making a point at a Pure Romance Board of Directors meeting in Puerto Rico in 2019.*

*My siblings (left to right) Nick, Lauren, Matt, and me with Patty in front at our warehouse in Loveland, Ohio.*

*The family gathers for a photo op at our Pure Romance 25th Anniversary celebration in Cincinnati. Left to right: Matt, me, Patty, Lauren, and Nick.*

*Cincinnati Mayor John Cranley declared one Saturday in April 2018 to be Pure Romance Day in honor of the company's 25th anniversary. Talk about making amazing strides!*

*Matt, Nick, me, and Patty after our Mount Union College squad won the 1997 National Championship.*

*Me and my family pose at the first Living With Change Gala in 2019. Left to right in front are Macie and Max. In back are my wife Jessica, our daughter LC, and me.*

*A product launch at the Aronoff Center for the Arts in Cincinnati in 2018.*

*Taking a stand at the opening of our Loveland, Ohio warehouse in 2009.*

*Back in 1984, when I was the little man of the family. Nick (age seven) is at far left with his arm around Matt (age two). I'm at near right (age nine) holding my sister Lauren (age one) close.*

*Me holding the boards during a Pure Romance training session in 2003.*

*It doesn't get much better than this. Here, I'm working from home in June 2020 during the COVID-19 pandemic surrounded by my kids (left to right) LC, Max, and Macie.*

*At the launch of my motivational podcast in 2019. It was rebranded at the beginning of 2021 as "The Secret is YOU with Chris Cicchinelli."*

*A Pure Romance Block Party held during our National Training in Cincinnati in 2019.*

*Leading a virtual consultant training session online during the pandemic, October 2020.*

*With my mother, Patty, and a life-sized bottle of Coochy shave cream during our National Training in 2018.*

# CHAPTER 8

# Confessions of a Realist

This is the chapter where I give you my opinion about the way the world works, and it has as much to do with my personal philosophy as with business. I know that the truth isn't particularly popular right now. A lot of people attack it and seem to relish the rejection of facts. But pragmatism is nonetheless the way I'm compelled to approach my life as a CEO, a husband, a father, a friend, and a mentor.

Yes, I'm a realist. Read on to discover what this could mean for your life.

I'll start off by stressing something that may seem obvious: *you* control your destiny. By this, I mean that if you perform certain actions and activities, if you have specific mantras, and if you live your life believing that the energy you put out into the universe comes back to you, then you can change your circumstances and be incredibly successful. That's the simple formula for having a better career and personal life. It certainly has worked for me.

One thing I struggle to convey to people is that you don't need a fancy degree to become a great success. In fact, the best thing I have going for me in terms of my business strategies is that I *don't* have a Wharton MBA, I *don't* have a Harvard MBA. I have a life MBA. I'm the best example of what I preach because I live it every day.

Practicing positive thinking and keeping a forward-looking attitude is more important than you can imagine. The difference I see between success and failure is so often wrapped up in self-conviction, in someone's believing they can do it. It sounds simple, but in truth it's the whole enchilada.

There are also a lot of things that drive me crazy that don't relate specifically to business life that I must nonetheless share.

Let's talk about one of my all-time pet peeves, which is the fact that we work so hard to spare kids' feelings about the harsh nature of competition, when in fact competition is designed in part to prepare them for some of the rougher aspects of the real world. The end result is, once those kids who are spared real competition grow up, they're not conditioned to strive to be the best but instead the same as everyone else.

Perfect example: in Little League Baseball, we want everyone to have the same amount of playing time. When I was a kid, not being good enough made you realize, "Okay, I've got to go home and practice, put in more time, get better." But now, we basically say to kids, "You don't really need to improve, because you're going to get the same playing time as Suzy and Betty and Jami regardless, because we want to be fair."

Oh, and even if you finish dead last, you still get a trophy just for participating, because heaven forbid having only winners receive trophies should lower your self-esteem.

Unfortunately, coddling does not work. It has never worked. All it does is set someone up for unrealistic expectations. Because let me tell you, there is no "fair" in business or in life. Fairness doesn't come into the conversation.

I mean, try to imagine the absurdity of coddling in business. It presupposes that if people are going to buy from one company, then they also have to buy from us. One for them, one for us. That's fair, right? No. Of course not. You have to win consumers over by being better than your competitor. It's Business 101. The playing field is never level; it's skewed to favor those who work harder, work smarter, and have a better product.

This is why when I tell you I'm a realist, it means I'm going to give it to you straight. I've learned a lot in two decades heading up Pure

Romance and training a few hundred thousand women to be their own boss, and one thing I've found is I'm doing everyone a disservice if I care more about their liking me than learning from me.

I'm going to tell you what I really think—not in a mean-spirited way, but in an authentic one. One thing I'll say right off the bat is that I don't believe you can work most effectively through conflict. Things must be dealt with and talked through. It's about communication. It's about respect. It's about honesty.

But one thing I'll tell you is I'm not here to add more Facebook friends or Instagram followers. If you want me to sit and lie to you and tell you selling is going to be easy, or you're not going to have to make phone calls and schedule networking meetings, you've got the wrong guy. There is no simple way. You're not going to thrive by playing more golf, doing more yoga, learning to be a better cook, or meditating more. No one in the history of business has grown their company by doing that.

Until the pandemic changed the whole dynamic, it had gotten increasingly difficult to attract and retain consultants at my company. There's a reason for that. Statistically, fewer people are starting to have a steady job early in their career. A lot of people are going to college later, going back to live at home after they graduate, and delaying their work-place launch in general. In the gig economy, for the millennials, the idea of putting in a full day's work has grown less important than lifestyle and leisure time.

When you're a business owner at Pure Romance, you're a lot of things. You're the employment manager. You're the rainmaker. You're the inventory manager. You're the human resources director. You're the sales and marketing person. Fewer and fewer people want that kind of responsibility nowadays. Anyone who is starting a business wears many hats; in the beginning, it's usually just a business of one, and that one person balances every aspect of it until they can grow it enough to add a team.

You're thinking, "Well, Chris, the alternative is just living paycheck to paycheck." And yes, that's pretty much the story we are seeing today. This is the first time since the Great Depression of the 1930s that a generation of workers will not earn at least as much as their parents did.

Employee retention isn't just a Pure Romance issue. It's a societal issue, and I think it's something the next generation is going to have to seriously look at.

The primary problem I see is that today's workforce isn't sufficiently driven. And if you're a coach, you have to work with the players you have. You can't be as hard on the millennials as you could be on my generation or the generations before. People often ask me, "Do you think the millennials are weak?" My answer is, "No, they just have a delivery mechanism that's inside their head, and they hear things the way they want to hear them."

Hopefully, I don't sound too much like an old dude ranting about how things were different in his day. But what's true is true.

Mind you, this isn't the case with *all* millennials. I've seen many who work their butt off and care more about achievement than acquiring every cool toy to validate their existence—and who don't suffer from entitlement issues. Unfortunately, it's the exception lately rather than the rule.

It isn't just that too many millennials are their own worst enemy. They also happen to be victimized by the worst job and economic prospects for any generation since the 1930s. They have taken on at least 300 percent more student debt than their parents did. They're only half as likely to own their own home as young adults were in 1975. One in five lives at the poverty level or below.

You know what millennials and too many others really don't want to hear? That they shouldn't keep going out and spending above their means. If you don't have it, don't spend it. That advice came directly from my grandfather. I've seen so many people build their businesses on credit with a puffed-up balance sheet and no cash or capital. It's the surest way to failure.

The average credit card debt in this country is $5,700. I'm guessing that the average reader of this book has less than $500 in their primary bank account. I don't want to see you out there buying more things that you really don't need, like a bigger home or a better car. I want to see you pay off what you owe first, then establish an emergency fund, and then build for the future. Then, after you do all that, if you want to pick up a few extras, sure, go ahead.

I can already hear you from here, screaming, "That's a boring lifestyle!" But I'm looking to make sure that you aren't heading for disaster later in life. I'm talking about when you're seventy and somebody from the government has to come in and change your diapers because you can't afford proper health care, you can't afford to eat properly, and you had to move back in with your kids because you spent money like it was going out of style and never saved. It bothers me a lot that not nearly enough people are having these conversations.

Trust me that this is a big, big problem. The truth is, I don't believe that nine out of ten people you meet are going to be able to truly retire. When I say that, I mean a healthy retirement in which they can live on what they've saved and take those extra vacations and don't need to supplement their income. Statistics tell us that based on current trends, many millennials won't be able to retire until seventy-five, if at all.

What we have here now is a global phenomenon. The average person is so caught up in influencer lifestyles, partying with their friends, going out, having cocktails, and living paycheck to paycheck that they don't put the proper attention to the future. I feel like I'm watching a very, very slow train wreck.

I'm not trying to be a doom-and-gloom type. Again, I'm just a realist. It used to be that people put a lot of attention toward building a retirement nest egg while they were able. Now, it's more like, "Hey, YOLO, baby! You only live once, right? Screw it, let's go to Tahoe, let's spend, let's enjoy. Then we'll come back and figure out how to save money." We're starting to see this attitude among those at the end of the baby boom generation. Being a responsible adult who looks at the big picture somehow has flown out the window.

The truth is that YOLO is bull. That's what I tell everyone who asks. Be smart. Don't spend every cent. Don't go out to dinner every night. Sacrifice some of your present for your future. It's what people with a brain do, because "I'll worry about it tomorrow" is not a plan. It's certain fiscal suicide.

Here is the good news: *you* have the opportunity to turn your personal ship around right now. It all starts with you. You are your number-one asset. You are the rainmaker for your own life, as I am for mine.

Think of yourself as a car that needs regular maintenance to perform at optimum efficiency and endure. You change the oil regularly. You get the car tuned up. You buy a new battery. You do the preventive maintenance to keep the car in tip-top shape for the long haul. And this also applies to your physical health, your dietary health, your mental health, and your financial health.

Most people don't understand that their mind is the single most important element they need to learn to control. It's the one thing they must have completely together when trying to launch a new business or live their life by design.

I see too many people wait too long to maintain and preserve all aspects of their health—physical, emotional, mental, and financial. They ask, "How did I get into this situation? I want to make a change." And that's great. The sooner the better. But what you need to understand is that it's *all* on you. You're the only person you're going to have to depend on for the rest of your life. You come into this world by yourself, and you'll leave it by yourself.

Is that harsh? Maybe. But it's necessary to drive home the point that no one is going to bail you out. You're *it*, baby. Accepting this fact requires coming to terms with the negative things your head may be trying to tell you—specifically, the idea that what you're believing and feeling is or is not "normal."

"Normal" is a loaded word. "Am I normal?" is one of the most common questions I get, along with, "Is there something wrong with me?" I don't claim to be a therapist, but it's easy to diagnose that behind the questions is the simple pursuit of validation.

The bottom line, of course, is that my normal is going to be different than your normal. There is a spectrum of what we believe to be normal, and if you fall anywhere on that scale—which I think is getting wider and wider—we think that's good. People just want to know that their insecurity isn't somehow peculiar. It's the certification of "You're okay."

*Consultant Spotlight:*
## Zara Zay (Part II)

*(Lives in: Ann Arbor, Michigan; twenty-six years in the business)*

"I can vividly recall my former life. I have been homeless. These were the days I was on government assistance to provide for my babies. When they were still very young, I would take my two little boys to the local thrift mart for a fun time and to buy their clothes. Ten years later, life was still pretty crappy.

"Once in a while, the hypertense madness of the past still haunts my dreams. I go back there. I'm a stressed-out waitress, standing on my head for an endless parade of hungry people. It was a living hell. I was forty years old, stuck in a steakhouse, working my butt off for the money.

"I always knew I had it inside of me to make my life better. I just needed a way to do life different. Thanks to Pure Romance, it all changed. For well over two decades, I have experienced travel throughout the world and been extremely fortunate to pay it forward to a list of charities. It has inspired confidence and belief in myself.

"Before the pandemic, I had a deep fear of speaking live on camera. I felt awkward and insecure. I avoided it like crazy. I even ducked cameras at corporate events. It was a phobia. When the world shifted into lockdown, I knew I had to embrace change—especially after learning of the super success enjoyed by my sister leaders using virtual party platforms. And as a bonus, these women and their customers were having so much fun!

"For the first time, I began to wolf down and study up completely on Facebook Live and Zoom platforms, because the world of in-home parties—forever my thing—was no longer an option. But Chris Cicchinelli offered a beacon of hope and nonstop Pure Romance trainings.

"To our great surprise, throughout the country and around the world, our businesses experienced extreme growth in 2020. Along with team members and the entire company, my expanded world embracing more social media skills has been game-changing. I can now relax with a video camera in my face. It's no longer paralyzing. I have even developed more verbally descriptive ways of communicating, because with virtual events, we can no longer rely on audience interaction and the ability to smell, taste, and touch.

"I can now go live on Facebook or Zoom at a moment's notice and chat it up with others. Fear of flopping has vanished. With virtual platforms, I can now connect more, broaden experiences, and strengthen relationships with team members and sister consultants."

There are more confused people out there than ever right now. They feel like they're not getting ahead fast enough. They're paralyzed by the division and strife and attempts to evoke perfection that they see on "Fakebook" and "Insta-Lie." These things cause people's self-confidence, self-worth, to plummet.

The end result is, too many people just pack it in. They throw in the towel not just on pursuing a career and a certain lifestyle but on the dream of owning their own business. Then they think, "I'm going to give up on taking care of myself." They can't find balance, so they capitulate on going out with their friends and give up on being the best possible daughter, mother, or sister. They allow it all to fall apart. It's a vicious cycle.

What matters most to me is the legacy I leave behind. It's important to me that I be remembered as someone who had grace, had class, had respect for people, and helped people develop as business owners and human beings. I'm not going to live hoping that in my next life, I'll be a better person. Instead, I'll be that person now and also help people to find the best version of themselves.

The most effective way for me to live my life by example is through my work ethic, something I take great pride in. You may outsmart me once in a while, but you'll never outwork me.

How did I develop my work ethic? Where did it come from? Well, I didn't want to be poor. Early on, there was a certain sense of desperation. My mother always says, "The most desperate people are the most successful," and I tend to agree with that. I didn't have anything growing up. We had to work hard for everything. No handouts.

I truly believe that your work ethic is something you have to instill in yourself. It doesn't happen automatically. You need to want achievement more than the other person, pure and simple. Personally, I like to win. I like to make stuff happen. My work ethic arose out of wanting all of that.

A work ethic isn't just about work, work, work, though. It's about knowing how to pace yourself. It's understanding how to change things up when you're sick to death of the grind. If I'm tired of the treadmill, I'll go run outside. If I've had it with the way my office looks, I'll change the way the tables are set up. It's all about getting myself back into the right mental space, which is honestly as important as how I'm feeling physically.

But consider yourself in the minority if you don't mind putting in the blood and sweat necessary to succeed at the highest level. I think I probably deal with that more than anything. Most people just don't like to work that hard. Quite frankly, very few want to put the effort in. Then again, if they did, everyone would be in the C-suite.

On the flip side of that is the fact that everyone wants to live comfortably, and too many go through life feeling the world owes them. One of my favorite observations is that you have to get comfortable with being uncomfortable. I understood early in my life that the only way I was going to make a good living was to do something nobody else wanted to do. That's where the money's at. And I knew I had to put everything I had into that effort.

When I was getting established at Pure Romance in my mid-twenties, my buddies were going to clubs, hanging out, watching football, and drinking. I never made it to one of those gatherings. Not a single one. To this day, my friends will be playing in their golf league, having a few beers, texting me, "Dude, why aren't you here?"

Every one of these guys thinks I work too hard. Fortunately, through trial and error, I have developed a personal Teflon that prevents people's negativity from sticking to me. And that's an incredibly important thing, because every one of us has, to some degree, fought that battle of worrying about what others think of us, what we should do, how we should live our lives—all of that.

If you allow others' perceptions of you to stick, they will have a tendency to grow and fester and keep you from maintaining your own positive sense of self. In my case, I was the shortest guy on the basketball team in high school and the smallest guy on the defensive unit on the football team. It fueled my drive and wound up inspiring me.

If you go into the sex toy business, it's crazy how much people want to give you advice and tell you what you can and cannot do. I endured a lot of that as a young man and had to quickly develop a thick skin.

It's taken a long time for me to get to where I am today as a man and as an emotional being. You always need to be strengthening your decision-making muscle and your mental acuity, so they're there when you need them to push you through the hard times.

Three years ago, you see, I hit a wall. A big one.

I felt I'd lost my creativity, and with it my drive. Have you ever just wanted to take a baseball bat to the computer in your office and leave it in pieces? That was me. I was so sick of hearing no, so fed up with my day-to-day, that I just couldn't take it anymore. So many people would look at a project or an idea and tell me why we couldn't do it. It was a parade of nos, or so it seemed. I was suffering from a lack of engagement. I was exhausted. I was burned out.

I tried to lay blame everywhere but where it belonged: on myself. Here I had been preaching that it was my job to create my own happiness, and now I couldn't do it. I was, in short, talking out of both sides of my mouth. I had to go back and figure out a way to make myself happy again, because I'd self-diagnosed a depression and anxiety disorder.

I had worked with performance coaches before, and I hired one again because I desperately needed to get unstuck. She sat me down and asked, "What is your base issue?"

"My biggest issue now is that I feel stuck and like I'm drowning in other people's problems," I replied. "I'll get done with a meeting and just feel like I can't keep everyone's issues from sticking to me. I don't have enough time to deal with everyone on the phone. I feel like I just can't do it anymore."

"Do you want to figure out why you're feeling this way?" she asked.

"Yes."

"Okay," she said. "Most of the stuff that we're going to deal with to explain why you act the way you act happened to you between the ages of three and seven."

And then she put me under hypnosis. She took me through a time-line from that day back into my childhood, so I became my five-year-old self again. I was five when my dad left, but I didn't specifically remember his leaving.

"Tell me what you see," she said.

We lived at the time in a bi-level house, and I just remembered sitting on the top level there screaming and crying. My mother was on the stairs, and my dad was walking out the door. I never saw that picture until I was under hypnosis; the subconscious will protect some of our most embedded memories and not permit them to be forgotten.

I awoke from hypnosis with the assignment to corroborate that story with my mom. And she did. It happened exactly the way I remembered it under hypnosis. I reported back in with my coach, and she asked, "Do you want to know why you behave the way that you behave?"

"I'd love to."

"It's because you will take on other people's stuff and say yes when you should say no. You'll agree because your fear of abandonment is so high, and because you don't want to feel the way you felt the day that your father left ever again. So, you'll take on everyone else's issues and they'll stick to you. But I'm sure you don't want to feel that way anymore."

Of course, I didn't. My coach told me that she was going to put me under hypnosis once more, and this time she'd be taking me from the moment when I finished on stage during one of my training sessions until I reached my car, "so you don't have to carry that baggage with you anymore."

So, I went back under. She guided me through a hypnosis session in which I literally had human excrement all over me. It was on my face. It was on my chest. It was on my shoulders. I got into a shower, turned on the water, and soaked it all off of me. Then I dried off and was immediately instructed to wake up.

"How do you feel?" she asked.

"I feel clean," I answered.

"Do you feel stressed?"

"No, I actually feel relieved."

Ever since that day, I've handled things differently, and it's mostly about my mindset. As soon as I'm done delivering a speech on stage, I imagine that my staff helps clean me up, and I mentally and metaphorically release to other people everything I've been carrying around. I never believed that I could do that before, because it felt like a sign of weakness. Now, I give myself permission to say that I don't have the bandwidth to carry everything around. All of the questions and issues that come in are now delegated to our core team. I learned that I couldn't handle fixing it all myself.

Why do I share this story? Because it's important that you not cart around the pressure to be omnipotent. Imagine feeling like you are responsible for the problems of some forty thousand independent consultants. Now, I make self-care a priority. I don't just preach it but practice it.

Some people just want to know they can have a conversation with you and that you actually care, that you'll look them in the eye and *listen*. It isn't about fixing anything. Sometimes, the best fix is for somebody to hear their own problem(s) out loud. The truth is that therapists are typically most valuable when they serve as a sounding board.

Now, I preface every interaction with one of our consultants by making it clear that I'd like to hear from those who need feedback, but their approach has to be constructive. More like, "Hey, I've got a quick question about something" rather than, "Oh my God, I've got a bunch of problems I have no solution to." You and everyone I work with needs to understand that you and they must be solution seekers. Have a possible answer in mind when you present an issue.

It isn't just in my business life that I can't practice being all things to all people. It's in my personal life, too. I have to limit myself to taking on one role at a time. When I'm at the office or on the road, I'm in the CEO role, in the provider role. I can't be in the parent role. I can't sit back and have this dad guilt that I can't always tuck my kids in at night, can't read books to them.

Instead of worrying, you have to be able to compartmentalize and do the work-life harmony thing. If I'm home with my wife and kids, I need to be happy and fully engaged with them while I'm there. Whatever role I'm in, I have to be there 100 percent and never halfway.

If you always go back to your purpose, it will help you get through the grind of the moment. I also try to practice gratitude through every step of the journey. When I've been on the road for three days and staying in a crappy hotel or sitting around an airport without having had a decent meal that day, I remember how lucky I am to have this life that I've carved out. It helps to recognize that there are people riding Greyhound, who need to hitchhike, or who live on the street. I'm very fortunate to be able to do what I do.

Look at your life as a gift, as I do mine. I get to be married to an incredible woman—my wife Jessica, who supports me wholeheartedly and lets me do what I need to do. She's my biggest fan. But at home, she's the boss. She's the CEO of the house, because I just have to fit in between business trips. I can't come in and shake everything up, which would prove very disruptive. That simply wouldn't be fair to my wife.

Jess is what I need in a spouse. She's my opposite. I'm up at five, sometimes six, working out. She's not a go-getter that way. I've got an intensity. I've got a plan. Jessica is far more chill. She's organized; she's patient.

I'd like to think I could run my business with as much confidence and grace as my wife runs our house and our foundation. Here is what I've learned about myself the hard way through the years, as spelled out so eloquently by the great author Brené Brown: "There will be times when standing alone feels too hard, too scary, and we'll doubt our ability to make our way through the uncertainty. Someone, somewhere, will say,

'Don't do it. You don't have what it takes to survive the wilderness.' This is when you reach deep into your wild heart and remind yourself, 'I *am* the wilderness'."

What is also undeniable is that you're that business. It's your business. That's why you put yourself on the line and invested your time, your energy, your money, your ego, your everything. If you're tough, you'll survive the difficulty and the uncertainty. But you really have to want it.

You have to be prepared, because 2021, and maybe even 2022 and beyond, promise to be very difficult years economically for a lot of people. The one unfortunate (or perhaps fortunate) thing that the pandemic and its resultant monetary nosedive have taught people is, if things go off the rails, there won't be many people (if anyone) there to catch you when you fall.

Remember: the secret is you, and *only* you. Don't expect anyone else to have your back. That's harsh, but it's the truth.

## Takeaways

- You have to work your way through conflict, because no one is going to coddle you in the business world. If they do, then you know that whatever you're involved in isn't worth the effort you're expending.

- You need boundless energy to succeed, so your best bet is to get serious about it now. Stop waiting. Get real. Understand that if you aren't willing to put in the work, you're always going to be strapped to a job where you're living paycheck to paycheck. That's a way to get by, but in no way will it feel like you're getting ahead. You have to believe you're worth the extra effort to make it.

- Pay off the things that you've purchased now. Don't live off your credit cards. What you want is to have the power of choice. Have an emergency fund. Go for the extras only after everything else is paid off. And make sure you create and regularly contribute to a retirement fund. I want you to be able to choose to work until you're seventy-five if you want to, but not because you have to.

# CHAPTER 9

# Call Me Coach

I make no secret of the fact that sports has played a huge role in shaping the person I am and the boss I've become. That influence goes back to high school and college. The people I learned the most from early on, and who showed the most interest in me, were coaches. They believed in me and what I could achieve even before I fully believed in myself, and that trust changed the direction of my life.

When I attended Mount Union College, we won two NCAA Division III national championships and went undefeated while I played for the varsity as a defensive back. We built something remarkable together while being made to understand that none of us had to be a superstar; we just had to each play our role.

I wasn't the most talented guy on the team or even close. But my coaches saw that I was passionate and would go the extra mile every step of the way. I made up in hunger what I lacked in natural ability.

Now that I'm a CEO, I have the same mindset that my coaches once had with me. Probably for that reason, I don't look at myself as a motivational speaker but as a coach. Like the football teams I played for, I have a goal every year at Pure Romance to get to the national championship game or the Super Bowl—that is, I have a strategy every day that moves us toward the optimum outcome. I work to utilize our employees to make sure I'm putting them in the best situations to win.

My daily goal is to make sure that I'm studying my competition. And by competition, most of the time it's not another company or product I'm talking about. The real competition surrounds keeping the culture inside our company proper and our people engaged and wanting to go to practice (to use the football analogy), which means doing the right things every day when no one else is watching.

There is a reason why our company has seen a consistent rise in revenue every year since I got here in 2000. It's because we treat our consultants like business owners. We deliver them solid and timely information. We instill confidence in them.

Let me just say that I'm a much better coach and leader today than I was, say, a decade ago. I run the company in a much different fashion now than I did in 2011, and it shows in the team we've built. Some people might say I was once an ass, particularly when I joined Pure Romance in my mid-twenties. I was twenty-seven when I started running the organization, and I think my expectations (of myself and others) were too high—due in large part to my own insecurities as a leader.

The difference for me today is that I don't just see our executive team and consultants as the means to a bottom line. My purpose is so much bigger than Pure Romance; it's to make sure that women in the room at our training sessions go out and live a better life. If that better life means $500 a month or $5,000, it's fine—it's all relative.

From where I sit, being a CEO and a coach very much line up, and every CEO has to have a little bit of head coach inside of them. What I mean by that is, CEOs need to coach people to do the right thing, to have more constructive conversations, and to come up with a game plan based on the type of people working for them.

As a CEO, you're constantly welcoming new people into the business and saying goodbye to others who are walking out the door. You're always dealing with a changing environment. While my job isn't to run everything and micromanage—which is the surest way to collapse—it does behoove me to understand a little bit about what everyone else is doing so I can best assist them in bringing their vision to fruition.

There are so many heading up companies who believe they need to be all things to all people. But I know, for example, that the product area has never been and still is not my strong suit. I'm getting better equipped to master our product line each day. However, we have sixty women on our senior board—the highest level you can reach as a Pure Romance consultant—and their job is to know a lot more about our products than I do. As a business leader, you want to put the right people in place and then trust them to do their job, or you shouldn't have hired them in the first place.

In the product area, I am tasked to listen to our research and development team members who make the product decisions and let what they say play out. At the same time, I recognize my most effective role and stick to it, and we're a better company for it.

Pure Romance is best served when I keep my eye on the big picture. And this is again where my sports experience comes into play. When things aren't working in sports, you don't keep doing the same thing; you change direction. At the same time, you don't necessarily look to do something drastic to alter the dynamic; you fine-tune. In business, you don't throw out the entire game plan because you had a bad sales quarter.

I've seen it happen so many times that as soon as things go a little bit south, the CEO panics. He or she starts seeking out advice from everyone. Like Chicken Little, they think, "The sky is falling! Oh no, what will we do?"

In the first quarter of 2019, when Pure Romance sales were down 17 percent, it was like a football team falling behind by two touchdowns in the first quarter. We had to figure out what was wrong and turn the ship around.

I had to tell our executive team, "Look, we're not going to panic. We're looking to change some things up. We're planning to get rid of some things. People are probably not going to be happy, but this is no time to coddle. This is real business."

See, I wasn't playing for the next two to three months, which most people would be strategizing about if they were publicly traded or cash-driven—if they had to satisfy shareholders. I was determined to play for a longer term. We planned that the turnaround would happen by year's end, and we weren't going to overreact. We plotted to ease into change gradually and commit to the same process that had gotten us to where we were. We were going to refine our approach, returning to the fundamentals and the basics that had worked in the past.

What we did to overcome our temporary tumble was simplify our consultant communications. We focused on activities that moved the needle and key thresholds, zeroing in on productivity and motivating our team. The one thing that was not permitted on my watch was freaking out. As a result, it turned out we were fine, and by year's end we were in better shape than ever.

But let's talk for a minute here about the elephant in the room in this age of #MeToo.

I've worked with close to 250,000 women during the past twenty-plus years, leading business development, operations, sales, and marketing for a company dedicated to empowering women to develop the necessary tools to become successful entrepreneurs. But yes, I am a man, sometimes the only man in the room. Guilty as charged.

How many times have I heard, "I can't believe we have a man as a CEO"? Probably a million.

The rest of the conversation might go as follows:

"Well, what does it matter what gender he is?"

"This is an intimate product. He can't possibly know what would make women want to buy it."

Here is how I answer that: I'm here to run a business. I'm also here to teach women how to operate their own gig within that framework. I'm guessing that anyone who won't take my advice would probably not take it from a woman in charge, either. As my mother frequently points out, whenever there is a strong woman presiding as the boss, the grumbling you frequently get is, "She's *such* a bitch."

Well, *why* is she a bitch? Is it because she has her act together? Because she's articulate? Because she understands everything that goes into keeping a business running? If she were a man, she would be called "capable" or simply "successful." The worst might be "tough."

Do some women have a hard time taking their marching orders from a man? Absolutely. And some women, and men, have a problem with being told what to do by anybody. We've all met those people. I see it in corporate America all day. What I can tell you in all honesty is, I don't speak to women any differently than I speak to men.

I think that once you start genderizing leadership and worrying about whether you're going to hurt feelings or not hurt feelings, you're in trouble. We can't be putting so much emphasis on where the message is coming from, and who it's aimed at, that we miss the content of said message.

The bigger issue I have is with inspiring people who need to change themselves to be able to evolve in business without receiving a detailed plan from me. And that's really about someone's getting past their own issues, insecurities, and challenges. If there is pushback on me for being a guy, or for my style, it's often more about getting to the root of what's going on inside someone's head that causes them to resist.

I'll admit that one of the toughest things I face as a CEO who wears so many hats is keeping up with our sales force. It's one reason I've averaged more than two hundred days a year on the road giving motivational seminars and training sessions, and meeting our team of independent consultants (that is, until 2020 and into 2021, when COVID-19 kept me anchored largely at home base).

The good CEOs, the smart ones, put in the time and energy to stay attuned to what their sales force is up to. I'm talking about guys like Jamie Dimon, chairman and CEO for JPMorgan Chase. He's one of the most successful businessmen in the world, but he felt he was losing touch with his culture. So, for the past ten years or so, he has gone on an annual bus tour of his branches, meeting with employees and customers to keep that connection with the rank and file.

My buddy Rob Lynch, the CEO of Papa John's, also has a plan, visiting the franchisees and the people delivering the pizzas; because at the end of the day, you're not going to find out what makes your company and culture tick from the boardroom. Rob took the seat after the company's controversial split with its founder. You have to get out there and talk with the people on the front lines.

A good CEO works hard to stay attuned to his or her people's wants and needs. Especially as a company grows bigger, a CEO winds up moving further and further from the culture they originally established, because there are now so many employees and potential layers of bureaucracy they need to work through. They're tasked with staying attuned to what's happening in the trenches.

One of my biggest shortcomings as a guy in charge is that I'm constantly having to remind myself to delegate. It has zero to do with not trusting the people I've hired and everything to do with being a control freak. You have to empower those around you to take responsibility and make decisions. They aren't always going to do things the way you want them done, but that's also how we all learn.

The understanding that I can't do this alone is what drives me to build the right leadership, sit back, and say, "Hey, if I want to take a month off and go with the family to Tahiti, I can." Of course, at the same time, I'm a little bit full of it, because I'd never feel comfortable enough to actually take a month off. (See again: control freak.)

Effective coaches and CEOs understand a few things pretty well. One is that it isn't them out there on the field but their players or employees. The second is that the most positive impact they can have on those they oversee is to inspire.

But the best part about being in charge of Pure Romance is witnessing firsthand how what we do helps customers improve their relationships and their sex lives. We've gathered the best people to brainstorm our product line and hand off the finest and most innovative merchandise of its kind ever created. From where I sit, it's a privilege to coach and teach and design and build. I love what I do.

It's also sometimes almost magical to witness the number of people who have come in here and didn't have two nickels to rub together, who had a massive amount of credit card debt, who were living in a cramped apartment with roommates or back with their parents, who then work hard and watch their lives change. I get to see them erase debt and buy their first home. It's a joy and a privilege to witness.

Our people here, if I train them properly, become agents of change in the world. That's why my own job is so important. You can't be looking for and worrying about glass ceilings. You have to believe you have the gift inside of you, and your job is to get it out and share it with the world— because the world is waiting.

If you look at our Pure Romance demographic breakdown, it's interesting to note that our independent consultant base is multiethnic and diverse in other ways as well. A survey launched at the beginning of 2020 found that nearly a quarter of our business owners are non-Caucasian (primarily Black, Hispanic, and Asian American) and relatively young (average age: thirty-seven).

They are also a well-educated bunch. Some 41 percent have a college degree. Virtually 100 percent have at least a GED, high school diploma, or technical school education. Nearly 6 percent have a master's degree or doctorate. (Yes, we even have several dozen doctors working as consultants, believe it or not—which comes in handy when discussing sexual health.)

For more than 80 percent of our consultants, Pure Romance is a side hustle (in addition to having another job or attending college). Working with us can help provide greater financial freedom. Maybe it gives women a small second income stream. Maybe it's simply a little something to do while the kids are in school. The beauty of it is, working here can be anything you want it to be.

Success at our company starts with a belief in the products we're selling. Why is this so essential? Because if you're representing something only to make money, you're not going to do terribly well at it. You have to have a core belief in your product line. I harp on the necessity of that every chance I get. Once you believe in what you're selling, you can start believing in yourself. One feeds the other.

When I got to the company twenty-one years ago, we had a sales force of around three hundred. Now it's over forty thousand. We didn't cultivate that growth overnight. It took time and patience. What it comes down to is, for the first time in their life, these women feel like they have someone in their corner who believes in them and has assured them they are worthy of getting more out of life. In turn, they have wound up believing there is more for them.

The story of my mother is important to relate, because it demonstrates to our consultants that she was once in their shoes. As a single mother earning $4.25 an hour, she struggled to put food on the table. Yet she made it big. We take pains to be sure our consultants understand that these things don't happen by accident but as the result of a whole lot of hard work. That's certainly how it came to be for her, and for me.

Concurrent to self-belief, there are two keys on the road to overcoming your self-doubts and making it happen:

- **Visualization.** See it in your head and you'll have faith in it. Look into your own private crystal ball, make incantations, and say out loud the things you want to have: "This is going to be a great day. This is my next step on the road to success." Not: "Oh, man. I've got only fifty bucks to my name and I suck. I'm not worthy. I'll never make anything of myself." What you say out loud, and what you believe inside, become self-fulfilling. You have the power to change your mindset and your circumstances.

- **Becoming a student.** You have to learn it to earn it. Remember: detach from your personal outcome, commit to the process, and success will happen for you. Becoming a student is one of the most powerful tools in your kit. It paves the road to achievement. Staying a student leads to greater accomplishment. You've got to keep learning during your entire life. I'm talking about being a student of your products, of how people behave, of how to interact, of understanding how to change, and of reading a room when you walk into it.

But in sports and in business, at nearly every company ever created, success always comes back to teamwork. That's what I believe, and that's what Shawn Achor believes.

Who is Shawn Achor? He's a *New York Times* bestselling author and one of the world's leading experts on the connection between happiness and success. He wrote a 2018 book that's become something of a bible for me: *Big Potential: How Transforming the Pursuit of Success Raises Our Achievement, Happiness, and Well-Being.*

I believe that Achor is growing into a world power with his ideas. He theorizes that survival of the fittest is a broken and backward system when applied to human success and happiness. He's found that when people work together, every metric of potential rises for everyone involved. In his judgment, teamwork matters most, above all other factors.

Another thing Achor has uncovered through his research surrounds the reasons teams have trouble focusing and functioning together in the workplace. Basically, it's this:

For the first twenty years of our lives, we are taught how to work independently, which seems to make sense. It's to prepare us for lives of self-sufficiency. So, everything we are shown and trained to do is based on individual performance. Once we get to high school, that individuality is supercharged in terms of classwork, grade point average, SAT testing—all of that.

We're trained how to behave by ourselves: "Look at how great I am! I'm going to undergrad at Harvard! I'm doing my postgraduate work at Stanford! Me! Me! Me! Alone! Alone! Alone!"

Then we finally graduate and hit the job market, and suddenly it's all about working with a team of people. And we end up having a very tough time because, heck, all our training was about being on our own. We don't work well with others because we were never asked to. If we had asked to work with people in school, it would have been called cheating. Now that we're grown-ups, it's collaboration.

It's no wonder that we run into all sorts of conflicts now in trying to work as a team. But for the next forty-plus years of our lives, everything is based on how well we perform with others. Fifty percent of our bonus is factored through how the company is doing, 20 percent on how we and our team function. It's crazy, right?

Could you imagine if we had been trained early on—from the age of, say, three—in how to actually collaborate with one another and call it cooperation rather than deception? How much better would we function as adults in our work lives if we had been furnished with that runway to learn how people most effectively work as a unit?

We're committed at Pure Romance to help our people get past the damaging lessons of their youth to thrive now. The most successful companies, by a wide margin, are the ones that embrace the value of collaboration and community.

Effective CEOs and coaches also recognize that 90 percent of the stress, fear, and anxiety in a job comes from 5 percent of the people. I can guarantee that as you just read that sentence, you were going through which of the people among that 5 percent to confront.

Succeeding with a team isn't necessarily about figuring out how to get rid of or bust the negative influences surrounding you. It's more a case of attacking the issue head-on by sitting down with the people and finding common ground. You might be amazed to learn how much you can discover about someone and rectify issues with a single face-to-face conversation.

Yes, I know. Actual discussion is such a quaint concept in this time of social media, social distancing, email, text messaging, and smartphones. But the best way to confront something, I have found, is to actually confront it. Don't let problems fester. Deal with something in a mature fashion and it can often be handled. The angst that the 5 percent of people create isn't fair to the other 95 percent.

The line between success and failure among office teammates tends to be a thin one. To a certain degree, we are all a little bit crazy. But the successful ones hide their craziness slightly better than the ones who aren't. That's what it's all about.

Another thing that I've found about the successful people on our team is, they're always willing to do the things nobody else wants to do. I think I mentioned that earlier in the book, but it bears repeating because it's so consistently accurate. High achievers do the team meetings when they don't feel like it. They make the phone calls when they don't feel like it. They do all those things because that's what gets them to the next level.

Imagine if I flew into a city for a training session and decided, "You know what? I'm not feeling it today. I think I'll leave those 350 women there by themselves and stay in my hotel room, watch the game, maybe order a pizza." I'll tell you what: if I ever do that, just go get the men in the white coats, because it'll mean I've lost my mind.

You want to know how else you instill respect in the people who work with you? Encourage feedback from *everyone*. You never know where the next great idea will come from, and a lot of our great ideas have come from those outside our executive team. Everyone who works at or with our company counts. Everyone matters. And they all know it. If they don't, I want to hear about it.

That said, I'll also go with my gut a lot. But before I do, I'll crowdsource. I'll open up a topic to the hive mind. There is a process I go through, and sometimes it makes sense to let some members of my team believe they're the decision-makers. Whether the outcome is good or bad, I'm going to live with it. I won't ever push it off on anyone else. The buck stops with me.

But I've got to say that I've grown pretty good at making decisions. I use the decision-making muscle a lot. It's like shooting free throws in basketball. If you practice something enough, you're going to get really good at it. There is no difference between shooting a free throw and making a decision. There is no difference between being a quarterback throwing a slant pass and making a decision.

It really does pay off in the final analysis, however, to give your people ownership. It inspires them to care that much more about every aspect of their job. Conversely, if you don't give them that responsibility, they invariably become completely reliant on you. Once they have the courage to stand up and be counted in the decision-making process, and they know that it's safe for them to do so, you as the CEO are no longer controlling the narrative. You're just approving.

I'm very pleased to walk into a room and be met with, "Chris, here is the schedule. Are you good with it?" "Yeah, it looks good." It may take a while to get to that point. But at every step of the corporate journey, empowering your people gives them the ability to grow and flourish.

We're in the place now at Pure Romance where my executive team and I have a shorthand. They understand what I'm looking for, and I get what they're capable of. This is the stage where real creativity and innovation can prosper, and when being a CEO or coach becomes incredibly simulating.

Then I go home and discover what a real boss looks like. My wife is the only person in the world I can't effectively coach—and I don't even try.

## Takeaways

- Cultivate the talent around you. It's a combination of motivation and nurturing. Point the way in a self-assured and confident way and your people will follow. Be the person who is steady in a storm, who leads with calm when a crisis comes. Those you work with will be inspired to emulate your example. I want my full team there to win with me.

- What you say out loud becomes self-fulfilling. It can sometimes be called fake it till you make it. If you utter something with conviction, even if you don't fully believe it inside, it can take on a life of its own. Pretty soon, you're believing it, and that belief is contagious.

- Winning by yourself is just plain not fun. Team leaders celebrating together makes all the difference. Everyone wants to be a part of something bigger than themselves, something that brings people together in service of a common goal. Rally behind that and watch magic happen in your business and your life.

# CHAPTER 10

# Winning Resides in Repetition

*"Repetition is the mother of learning and the father of action, which makes it the architect of accomplishment."*

—ZIG ZIGLAR

There is no more important quote in the history of commerce than the above. Quite simply, repetition is fundamental to the success of any sales business. Let me repeat that to drive home the point: *repetition is fundamental to the success of any sales business*. In fact, it's key to any business, period.

Success happens *because* of repetition. There is a long, boring history of repetition behind the way a city runs, the way a car model is put together, the greatness of a top athlete, a brilliant actor, and a well-run country. It's the grunt work behind the scenes that brings it home, the monotonous practice that makes perfect.

You may be jealous when you see someone worth millions or billions who is working and delegating behind a laptop while staying at a resort, the waves crashing in the background. What you don't see are the years and decades when that person worked harder than everyone, sacrificing to get ahead, putting in twelve- and fourteen-hour days—doing the same thing over and over.

Repetition.

Being successful takes practice and practice and more practice. Repetition. Much of it is just plain tedious. But if you want to make success happen for yourself, you're going to have to get cozy every single day (including weekends) with the repetitive work that it takes to become an expert. A big part of what I teach as a CEO is how to grind it out, persevere, and add repetition to your daily routine. This is what it looks like for me.

| Chris' Pre-COVID Schedule | Chris' COVID Schedule |
|---|---|
| 5:30 a.m. Workout | 5:30 a.m. Get up/coffee/news |
| 7:30 a.m. Operation phone call | 6:30 a.m. Workout |
| 8:00 a.m. Flight to location | |
| 9:00 a.m. Emails and text messages on flight | 7:30 a.m. Emails and calls to executive team |
| 9:30 a.m. Land, make calls to salesforce leadership | 8:30 a.m. More coffee/ "Rise and Grind" prep |
| 10:00 a.m. Calls with marketing, training, and accounting | 9:00 a.m. "Rise and Grind" with consultants |
| 12:00 p.m. Lunch on the fly | |
| 2:00 p.m. Meetings with local leaders | 9:30–10:30 a.m. Executive meeting |
| 4:00 p.m. Quick workout before meeting | 11:00 a.m. Creative meeting |
| 5:00 p.m. Calls with kids and Jess | |
| 6:30 p.m. Meeting starts | 12:00 p.m. More meetings |
| 9:00 p.m. Meeting ends. Pictures and socializing with attendees | 5:00 p.m. Another meeting/drinks |
| 9:30 p.m. Dinner with local leaders | 7:00 p.m. Family dinner |
| 10:45 p.m. Back to the hotel | |
| 11:30 p.m. Check up on email | |
| 12:00 a.m. Lights out | |

*Credit: Shadow Woolf*

As you can see, I put in the time. I'm going constantly. I don't just preach it; I also live it.

Now here is what some of the wealthiest Americans do daily to put repetition first. All net worth numbers are approximate and were current as of the time of this writing in 2021.

### Sara Blakely

*Net worth: $1.1 billion*

The founder of the shapewear and leggings company Spanx starts her day with yoga at 6:30 and follows that with the exact same breakfast every morning: frozen wild blueberries, a few dark cherries, kale, dates, cinnamon, spinach, cilantro, fresh mint, lemon, water, ice, chia, and walnuts. At the office, Monday is her think day, Wednesday her meeting day, and Thursday her time with the product and creative team. After a full day at the office, Blakely picks up her kids from school, gets home, and unwinds with a warm bath.

### Jeff Bezos

*Net worth: $197 billion*

The world's second-richest man rises (without an alarm) after sleeping for eight hours, then spends his mornings reading the paper, sipping coffee, and eating breakfast with his family before heading to Amazon headquarters. His mornings are filled with meetings beginning around ten o'clock. He tries to keep his afternoons flexible and always includes a workout. After work, he has dinner with his family and, notably, washes the dishes.

### Elon Musk

*Net worth: $208 billion*

Now the world's richest man, the CEO of Tesla and SpaceX rises at 7 a.m. and skips breakfast. He responds to emails and spends time with his six kids before showering and heading to work at SpaceX headquarters in Los Angeles (Mondays and Fridays) or at Tesla in the Bay

Area (Tuesdays, Wednesdays, and Thursdays). He divides his day into five-minute blocks, including a wolfed-down lunch.

## Bill Gates

*Net worth: $134 billion*

The Microsoft cofounder and former CEO usually skips breakfast and hits the treadmill before reading the news. Like Musk, he divides his day into five-minute blocks, conducting a series of meetings and reading in between. His nightly ritual is doing household chores in his $154 million mansion, even though it would seem a house that expensive should clean itself.

## Warren Buffett

*Net worth: $88.2 billion*

The chairman and CEO of Berkshire Hathaway and renowned philanthropist sleeps for eight hours and gets up at 6:45 a.m. sharp. He then heads to his local McDonald's (yes, McDonald's) for breakfast and coffee. At the office, a good part of Buffett's day is spent reading and taking meetings. After work, he sits down for a vigorous game of bridge and practices the ukulele.

## Mark Cuban

*Net worth: $4.4 billion*

The tech billionaire, *Shark Tank* investor, and owner of the NBA's Dallas Mavericks rises to a morning routine of having decaf coffee and Alyssa's Cookies, reading email, and watching CNBC. He adjusts his schedule around his children's school, avoiding meetings whenever possible. When not out watching his beloved Mavs, he puts his kids to bed and exercises on an elliptical for an hour.

The bottom line here is that these leaders who have risen to the very top have routines that they rarely vary from, and that repetition helps keep them in tip-top shape for the grind ahead.

But repetition also has an important function in every aspect of the business world. Take, for instance, marketing and advertising. Repetition is what makes you choose one product, one style, one idea, one movie, or one brand over another (or many others), embodying the power of persuasion. It's effective and it's proven. To test the theory, all you need to do is look at these slogans and see how long it takes for the products associated with them to pop into your head:

- "Just Do It."
- "Think Different."
- "Breakfast of Champions."
- "Have It Your Way."
- "It's Everywhere You Want to Be."
- "The Ultimate Driving Machine."
- "Because I'm Worth It."
- "Fly the Friendly Skies."

If you're of a certain age, you're going to instantly know the companies I'm talking about. In order they are: Nike, Apple, Wheaties, Burger King, Mastercard, BMW, L'Oréal, and United Airlines. Do you think the mind-sticking aspect of these brand-recognition phrases happened by accident? No. It's the result of tens of millions (maybe hundreds of millions) of dollars and impressions designed to attach these slogans to your cortex.

Repetition. Repetition. Repetition.

It's been proven that it pays off in a greater way to email the same two thousand qualified prospects twelve times than it does to email twenty thousand or twenty-five thousand prospects once or twice. The volume and repeating of the message are what seal the deal.

Research also finds that consumers need to be exposed to a message seven times (the famed "rule of seven") before they decide to purchase something. Frequency, it has been proven, breeds familiarity. Familiarity ultimately becomes trust. Trust is what spurs buying.

How does this factor into your own life? It's all about having a routine that you follow tirelessly and relentlessly. We all know people who flop from job to job, who never seem to have the ability to stick with anything, right? If they're in sales, it doesn't matter which company is next in line, because they haven't figured out that it's never the business that fails. They are the ones who failed the business.

If this sounds like you, listen up. It's happening because you don't have a productive routine. You haven't gotten into the repetition habit. You've not been able to put it into action. If you want to be a great speller, writer, basketball player, or ballerina—whatever—you have to do the thing over and over and over again until you get it down perfectly. Then you must enhance your routine.

That enhancement is equally important in the repetition game. You don't simply do the same thing and never change it up. It's about finding what works, incorporating it, and tweaking it a little bit, tinkering, perfecting. If I'm writing a sentence in this book, maybe I want to put a little more emotion into it to make it really sing. That is how you win.

I built a business on repetition. I've been on the road as much as 250 days in a year, going out and doing the same thing. That's how I expanded my business. There is no secret sauce. I'm not smarter than everybody else. I just did the work, over and over.

Repetition. It's like shampooing your hair: lather, rinse, repeat.

Those I train on the road can take everything I teach them and apply it to whatever they do in life. Whether that's to Pure Romance, their current job, or their secondary job, none of the training is proprietary for promoting a direct sales business. It isn't about teaching them how to sell a product but how to sell themselves. *They* are what people are buying. They are in essence marketing their brand.

The investor, entrepreneur, and author Gary Vee talks about his routine. He's mega-successful, yet he's still the hungriest guy out there. He will wake up at three in the morning and go to bed at eleven at night, then start all over again the next day.

Now, I'm not advocating that you turn into a crazed workaholic and sleep four hours a night. The point is that this guy has become legendary in the motivational and investment communities because he has this routine that he doesn't vary from.

If your kids want to get better at something, you're going to tell them to do the routine because every move they make matters. Every one of us is our own trusted brand. Particularly in a world where all of us walk around with our own video recording and social media publishing capabilities in the palm of our hand, we're constantly onstage. Justin Timberlake, Taylor Swift, Beyoncé, they're all about routine and making sure they stay on message.

I get that everything I do as the President and CEO of Pure Romance is going to be scrutinized. I'm a very driven guy, but my drive came through repetition. You know what repetition is? Every time you go to the gas station and you need to scrounge together change to pay the cashier for your gasoline, that's the repetition of being broke. I didn't like the feeling of needing that change to make ends meet. I decided that was a repetition I didn't need anymore, so I went out and found a new one.

Now, I don't even have to scrutinize the bill when I'm in a restaurant. That's freedom. I built that through my repetition, through my constant vigilance to advance myself and grow our company's footprint, our brand. It was my behavior of going and going and going and refining and going and refining some more.

Do you think that without repetition, LeBron James would be as great as he is today? I mean, he'd be good; don't get me wrong. Just based on his physicality, being such a specimen, and his pure ability, he would be a solid NBA player, maybe even a superstar. But he wouldn't be one of the two or three greatest professional basketball players of all time.

(If I may add an aside here, author Jim Collins has said, "The enemy of great is good." Today, I encourage you to remove the word "good" from your vocabulary. You don't want to have a *good* team; you want to have a *great* team. You don't want to have a *good* business; you want to have a *great* business. You don't want to have a *good* marketing plan; you want to have a *great* one. Good is a cop-out. Great is always the goal. But I digress.)

The difference with LeBron—why he is no ordinary superstar but maybe the finest basketball player who ever laced up—resides in his drive and routine. He has repetition in the weight room. He has repetition in his diet. He has repetition in his shooting routine. He never stops or slows down. He pushes, pushes, pushes, and he doesn't vary what he does. That's what sets him apart.

You see some really amazing athletes who get to the NBA and have a great routine and repetition. They're super talented. They get paid the big bucks. Then they start to get comfortable and let themselves go, and they stop working so hard. They break their routine. They sleep in. They stop pushing as much because they think, "Screw it. I'm already doing good. I don't need to drive myself so hard anymore."

Dennis Rodman was never satisfied. Kobe Bryant was never satisfied. Michael Jordan played three sports, never satisfied. Satisfaction leads to complacency. It's what should happen when you retire, not when you're out trying to slay dragons in the world. Complacency is what losers feel. Winners keep plugging away at their routine and don't break from it just because a little success comes their way.

Repetition. It's the whole ballgame.

Do you stop going to the hair salon because you figure you've already done that before, so you're good now forever? Do you stop being concerned about your physical health because that's gotten old? Hopefully not. Presumably, staying healthy and looking your best will be a lifelong commitment you've made to yourself.

The way you sell yourself is an important part of a necessary routine and repetition. Did you know that 55 percent of the way you communicate is through your body language? Body language is the biggest thing in communicating. People are watching you, consciously or unconsciously, to see if you're confident, the way you walk into a room, your facial expression, if your shoulders are back or slouched over, if you look people in the eye.

### Consultant Spotlight:
### Katy Ross

*(Lives in: Perth, Western Australia; eleven years with Pure Romance)*

"Bedroom accessories were a very new thing in Australia when I started ten years ago. It's opened me up to a whole new world and surprised me that so many people need our products. As consultants, we provide an experience and service like no other, and can genuinely help women and couples.

"Pure Romance has been my primary source of income more or less from the beginning. I saw the money coming in pretty quickly and was making more doing one to three parties per week than working my three jobs combined, so I made a goal to go full time within a year after starting. I wound up taking the plunge six months in and never looked back.

"What I love about this job is the way it constantly gets me out of my comfort zone. All great growth in life comes from pushing yourself beyond limits you thought were possible, so I make sure not to get too comfortable, and constantly challenge myself. I also love the friendships, the money, the travel, the fun, the lifestyle, and how I can take time off whenever I need to.

"I always make sure to do something every day that touches my business, whether it be booking and holding parties, making team connection calls, connecting with my hostesses, selling products, or talking to my leads.

"How has being a Pure Romance consultant changed my life? Let me count the ways! I've seen money I could barely have dreamed about a decade ago. I've met amazing women, traveled the world, created lifelong memories, experienced amazing cultures, and purchased my dream home with a goal of paying it off within five years (twenty-three years early). All of that, and of course the epic life skills this job has imparted.

"The pandemic has made me appreciate my business even more. It's been a blessing in disguise. Who knew we could do online as well as in-person parties? I love that I can choose whether to work from home or go out and party."

We automatically believe that most communication happens through words. Not so. Not even close. Words themselves are actually only 7 percent of communication, with tonality and how we speak accounting for 38 percent. A big part of what I teach is coming across confidently in style, tone, and body language, and then repeating it over and over.

This speaks to our whole strategy at Pure Romance in bringing consultants into our fold. We take individuals who may be working at a restaurant, working retail, or maybe employed as an administrative assistant, and turning them collectively into successful sales teams. How? We teach them the skills of repetition, one small step at a time.

Each year, we see a subtle decline in "soft" selling skills, basically social skills. We are now a society that communicates in 140 characters or less. It's become necessary to really teach people how to have a conversation, how to form an introductory speech—what's sometimes called an elevator pitch. Our strategy in the beginning is really about refining that for them.

If we don't figure out how to help them say this stuff to their friends and family members, the Pure Romance business kit they bought is basically going to remain in the closet. We have to make sure their scripting is done properly. Very few of us are born salespeople. Selling is a skill that must be taught—over and over, repetitively—until they get it right.

We also make sure our consultants understand that they're creators of experiences, not simply sellers of products.

Particularly at first, we get a lot of excuses over effort. So many of the newbies tell me the reasons they can't go out and work or build relationships with the people who attended their parties. The biggest obstacle people have to overcome is themselves. The best way I've found for them to do that is to establish a routine early on. Commit to the process, detach from the outcome.

But at the same time, all repetition needs to be an evolving beast. You can't stay stuck in a cycle that's outdated or antiquated, and you must constantly refresh your routine.

For instance, at my company we're bringing a new piece into our ecosystem by giving our products a medical facet that shows women

Pure Romance isn't just about fun and recreation. It's about the entirety of their sexual health and wellness. We're looking at different delivery mechanisms as well.

Right now, I don't think our in-home party plan is an old model. There are always going to be face-to-face sales in a home environment. Certain customers will forever prefer to buy that way. At the same time, we've learned that we need to be flexible and forward-thinking in how we approach the future for the end user.

I mean, look at a corporation like McDonald's. When it started, you walked up to the counter and paid for your burger and fries. Then a drive-through window was added in 1975. Later it was, "Hey, let's add sit-down service." Now, you put in the order yourself at a kiosk. It's the same hamburger, the same fries, and the same Coke; it's just a different way of delivering them to you. It's an evolution.

Amazon is creating drones to drop off Prime purchases to customers. The company had already tapped FedEx, UPS, and the U.S. Postal Service and needed to enhance its delivery options. It does so much business that it needed to move to a seven-day delivery model. Then it had to tap into Uber, Lyft, and Postmates drivers to get products to people.

Now you have Pure Romance looking into different distribution methodologies and mechanisms to deliver things to the customer in a more efficient fashion. We're also taking a look at ways we can maybe start personalizing somebody's experience. It could involve their own music selection and facial recognition as well as using our product line to define the customer experience at every stage of their personal development.

I don't believe that our ultimate distribution system for Pure Romance is going to be via in-home parties. This is why we've built out our ecosystem to accommodate more people, more demographics, more variety in the types of buyers we serve. It's also why we're focusing on creating an innovation lab that modernizes our product line through outside-the-box thinking.

We're dedicated to taking risks in the same way that Amazon has with drones, to stay ahead and deliver what customers want even before they know they want it. We're going to find the best possible things, plug them into our mechanism, and create a network that brands us as having great products, great partners, and some of the best technology and innovation in the sales universe.

How does this tie in with routine and repetition? It's about evolving on the fly and fueling an ever-changing procedure. We've gotten a taste of this during the COVID-19 crisis, because traditional in-person, in-home Pure Romance gatherings were no longer possible. We made a choice to drive a different model that wound up working beyond our wildest dreams, but that's because we were open to the idea of having a duplicable process.

We already were determined to do business in 2030 outside booking in-home parties. We have been training our consultants to sell products using different avenues online, including making virtual parties an option for their clients. We were looking to incorporate multiple selling platforms. We were simply forced to implement this earlier than we'd planned

One way we've progressed of late is to create a new touch-sensor type of product without buttons; you just kind of swipe left or right to operate it. That's new; that's innovative. That's the kind of stuff we intend to bring to the market in an increasingly pioneering way.

Evolving is a form of repetition. We are consistently changing the packaging on even our most popular products, because we aren't interested in being Borders or Blockbuster or any of the other companies that didn't see the need to change their look or system with the times, that thought sticking with the tried-and-true was going to be their ticket to forever. Innovation is the key to long-term success.

It's so easy to become outdated and obsolete. It's as simple as siting on your hands. When I say "routine and repetition," advancement and growth are part of that. You keep repeating different things, not the same things.

I'll give you a perfect example. It would have been incredibly easy for my mother to simply go with the flow once she started our business in 1993. The products, then known as "marital aids," were marketed *by* men *for* men. Part of the reason for that was, no one thought there could be another way, if for no other reason than sexuality itself had been controlled by men going back to the caveman era.

Sex was a very male-dominated topic in general. It was basically a societal thing. Men would get together and talk about brothels and strip clubs. Everything that was sexually oriented was designed to serve them. So why would anyone think it could ever be different?

Well, my mother did. She imagined herself, as a woman, doing the shopping for lubricants and lotions and gels and vibrators. That's why she demanded that the naked pictures of women be taken off the packaging. She knew that women were the primary consumers of the products, and they should therefore be targeted in the marketing. This strategy is simple Business 101 in hindsight but was revolutionary a quarter century ago.

It's really no wonder why Pure Romance became the go-to for intimacy products. We understood better than anyone who our customer was, and in general it wasn't men. It was women who were bored when it came to their relationships and were curious about how to integrate something other than the same old vanilla ice cream to spice things up.

The way we did it was by putting women and repetition first. We operated with proper terminology that played into the idea that our products were classy, not dirty. We led with education and sophistication. We worked incredibly hard—with a repetitive mantra, if you will—to eliminate the negative connotation of what we and our products represented.

I'll give us credit for doing the lion's share of switching around the perception. We see the same thing happening today with cannabis and CBD. Cannabis purveyors sold the idea that there is a medical benefit to these products in fighting the effects of chemotherapy for cancer treatment in particular, that they could help you with any variety of ailments and conditions from anxiety to chronic pain to symptoms of MS. Cannabis and CBD stopped being part of this evil "reefer madness" thing that supposedly was going to take down mankind, serve as a gateway to all sorts of harder drugs, and so forth.

If you had commissioned a poll twenty years ago about weed and public perception and then another one this year, the difference would be astonishing. You have states legalizing the sale of it even for recreational use now. It's a complete one-eighty from the way it was.

There has been a similar perceptual evolution for sex toys. They had long been seen as somehow shameful or sleazy, and if you used these products there had to be something wrong with you or your relationship. Not anymore. Now, they are considered a positive part of a healthy physical connection and of sexual health and awareness.

With bedroom toys, as with marijuana, perception is steeped in the repetition of the message. The messages about both ultimately have become so ingrained in the public psyche that it's grown difficult to remember a time when the thinking was so very different.

This is not to say that marijuana and intimacy products are approved by everyone. Not even close. But we're making all sorts of headway that was long thought inconceivable. At Pure Romance, we have successfully articulated the benefits of what we create and market with the mission to continually educate the consumer.

At the same time, we don't argue with those who oppose us. We simply explain who we are and allow word of mouth to spread. If ten people love the Pure Romance experience at a party, each of them tells ten more, then each of those tells ten more, and pretty soon the message has grown exponentially—through repetition. This repetition has made our fight for respect a lot easier. Now, we're dealing with a perception problem not with the masses, but with only a comparative few.

That is not to say the battle has been anything close to easy. It's been a journey of not giving in when it would have been easy to throw in the towel many times. We could have quit when people ran us out of different states, or when an ignorant minority held us up as the butt of jokes. But we didn't. We kept pushing forward.

What is most gratifying today is how intertwined what we sell is with information about women's bodies, health, sexuality, and awareness, which also ties in with the #MeToo movement. Sexually oriented products are intrinsically connected with women's owning of their sexuality today.

Every bit of that advancement is fed through the message of repetition. Repetition wins the race. Every time.

The other thing you have to constantly be aware of, as discussed, is the necessity of embracing change, and you must be willing to grow with the change. Change creates stress and anxiety in most people. You have to deal with the change of environment that's going on around you. This is a key thing to remember for women business owners, who as a rule don't like change. It's one more thing to learn and get adjusted to. But another word for it is evolution.

While change is inevitable, growth is optional. Once you accept that idea, it becomes much easier to deal with it, because then you're prepared for it. You know it's coming.

Make change part of your routine, part of your process, and you're in the driver's seat. Conversely, when you lack a process, lack a routine, lack repetition, you're done. Process is a necessary component, what I like to call the vanilla frozen yogurt of your career life. You practice it and refine it until it becomes second nature, until it's ingrained in who you are—until you no longer even have to think about it.

I talk about vanilla froyo as being the embodiment of routine and repetition. You have a great big bowl of it, right? But you also have the option of adding flavor to it, because there is a huge selection of crushed Oreos, Snickers, Heath bars, and cheesecake things. It's the same with a routine.

Think of the frozen yogurt bar as life itself, as the elements that can make your business life exciting and challenging every day. Finding someone in your routine who will make cold calls with you is like adding Oreos to your froyo. Another week, maybe you go to a networking group. That's like putting on gummy bears.

The idea is to always be adding small things to your routine that will keep it fresh and lively, that will prevent it from growing hopelessly stale. The boredom is why people quit following a routine. They chuck it because they don't find the gummy bears. In fact, if I write another book, I'm probably going to wind up calling it *Who Took My Gummy Bears?*

Life will be sweeter when you look forward to tackling each new day while doing what you love. The secret is staying hungry, exercising repetition...and eating gummy bears.

The bottom line is this: do whatever you need to do to hold your attention and keep your routine and life interesting. Ladle on a spoonful of sugar to get the kids to eat their peas or broccoli. It's the same idea with a routine. As Nike tells us, just do it. Do it every day. Stay focused. Stay aware. Keep your eye on the ball.

Also, there is no right or wrong when it comes to a routine. A lot of people ask me, "Why do you stay at the same hotel every time you're in town? Why do you eat at the same restaurants?" My response is, "Why did Steve Jobs always wear a black turtleneck and jeans every day? Why does Mark Zuckerberg stick to his gray T-shirt?" It's about establishing a habit. Why does the brain need one more thing to think about? We already have enough options that require our engagement.

Zig Ziglar's quote that opened this chapter bears repeating here at the end: "Repetition is the mother of learning and the father of action, which makes it the architect of accomplishment." It's been shown that forming effective habits depends on how often a person does something, not how much they enjoy it. Of course, I also have to believe that enjoying it helps, too.

At the same time, the secret to mastery in any task or human endeavor—from sales to surgery, athletics to music, phone calls to speechmaking, manufacturing an automobile to constructing a house—is repetition. It may not be sexy, or thrilling, or particularly fascinating, but it embodies the necessary effort that paves the way to success.

There are no shortcuts or apps that will bail out your lazy butt. You just need to roll up your sleeves and get to it. Over and over. You'll thank me later.

## Takeaways

- One of the greatest times of my life was when I played football in college. We were playing to win every play, every series, every quarter, and every game. And because we did that, because every single play counted, we won two national championships. That's what you have to do in your work life. Make every hour of every day count. Put out maximum effort every moment. No skating by.

- Sacrifice and grind is what it's all about, over and over. Winners keep plugging away at their routine and don't break from it just because a little success comes their way. Repetition is what supplies the fuel. It's about not stopping. Ever.

- You are what people are buying. The product is just the expression of your brand. And remember the marketing "rule of seven," which dictates that a prospect needs to be exposed to your message at least seven times before they'll take action to buy that product or service you're offering. That's your personal brand at work.

- I don't believe in a work-life balance. I have to create my own harmony, and it's not always harmonious. Sometimes, I get stuck in a different mode, but I work to repeat the things that have worked for me before. I built a great business on repetition. There is no secret sauce; I'm not smarter than everybody else. It's just doing the work, over and over.

# CHAPTER 11

# Making a *You*-Turn During a Pandemic

Now that we have the benefit of hindsight, it's clear that my company not only has survived the great COVID-19 pandemic of 2020 but is somehow thriving. I write this not as a boast but with a humble measure of disbelief, if not outright astonishment.

Think about it. We are a company whose sales are—*were*—generated almost entirely through in-home parties. But beginning in March of 2020, the state of Ohio (where our world headquarters is based) was locked down, as were most other states in the U.S. By the middle of that month, the federal government followed guidelines from the Centers for Disease Control and Prevention urging the public to avoid social gatherings of ten people or more.

This was, on paper, a nightmare scenario for us. We were essentially told that our entire business model was, at least for the short term, obsolete.

But let me back up for a moment.

Since January 2020, I'd been looking at that twelve months as a year of discovery, having eyed the future at the Consumer Electronics Show in Las Vegas. It convinced me that personalization and online sales experiences were the wave of the future, and that the future was really just months away.

But I knew after returning from CES that we had to be more proficient in our online business and work on doing a better job with virtual parties and maximizing the customer experience over the internet.

Then came March, and everything instantly changed.

As I recall it, the first meeting after lockdown wasn't, "Oh crap, what are we going to do now?" but, "We need to transform this business right now. It's not an option." This was the message we knew we needed to convey to everyone in our universe, that we were going to figure out a way to turn the ship around before hitting the iceberg.

We had consultants who were initially freaking out, for sure. They basically fell into three groups:

**Group One:** *"All right, I've got to change how I run my business. Time to pivot."*

**Group Two:** *"Oh my God, I'm paralyzed! I've only done home parties. This is going to be too hard. I'm not really technologically savvy. I don't know what to do. My whole business is going to melt. It's over!"*

**Group Three:** *"Oh no! I'm going to stay home. I'm going to follow the protocols. I'm done with this business. COVID is all over my boxes. I'm never going to touch one of them again. I'm going to leave everything from Amazon out on the street for nine days, because the virus lives on that stuff."*

Here is what I knew going in: if you give people the opportunity to really flip out and panic during a crisis, they will. That's the thing we didn't do. We moved quickly. As soon as we knew what we were up against, we didn't stop. We didn't give our people time to consider all the things going wrong. We didn't give them time to process, because in this case, process would have meant paralysis.

Yes, of course they were overwhelmed and scared to death that their livelihood was going away. But I didn't have the option to panic. As a leader, I made sure I had it all together and conveyed a sense of calm and confidence. Was I anxious inside? You bet I was. There were moments when I wondered, "Are we going to get shut down? Are they not going to let us ship orders?"

I went through the whole gamut of emotions. But I didn't show it. I knew that if I revealed to our consultants that I was panicked and upset, they would parrot it back to me. They reflect the mood of the leader. So I needed to stay strong. I wanted them to think, "Well, Chris is okay, so I guess it's all going to be fine."

At the same time, I naturally understood everyone's concerns about how an in-home party could translate to an online party. I knew the arguments all too well: "But Chris, I've got to pass the products around. My customers need to smell it, touch it, taste it, feel it, experience it."

My response was, "Well, you're just going to have to be a better storyteller now."

What I was basically tasked with was guiding everyone in essentially going from broadcast TV to Netflix overnight. For the lockdown period and essentially all of 2020, we were going to be the equivalent of a streaming service. But where some people have struggles, others find opportunities. I was determined to uncover those, because we can't control our conditions; we can control only our choices. It's a maxim that I live by.

We successfully managed to flip a switch and transition in a two-week period from being a company with a plan based on in-home parties to one with a virtual-party blueprint. During April and May 2020, nearly 100 percent of our parties were held over Zoom and Facebook Live.

How did we do it? For one thing, we didn't hesitate. We didn't write a business plan. We didn't sit back and think about it and say, "We need to have all our ducks in a row and dot every 'i' and cross every 't' before we act." We didn't analyze the heck out of it through focus groups. We just winged it by trusting our gut—primarily *my* gut.

Remember the three groups of consultants I mentioned? After the second week, the first group was off to the races. The second group had changed their tune to, "This technology thing isn't that bad. I'm starting to get the hang of it." The third group was, "Oh my gosh. I'm still paralyzed.

You guys shouldn't be doing anything. We all need to be washing our hands constantly and drinking Listerine straight."

By the third week, the first group was totally killing it, kicking butt on Zoom and Facebook Live. The second group was, "Hey, I'm flying." And the third group started coming around. It was, "Okay, it's not that bad. It's not the Apocalypse." And the reason the new plan worked was that we were all in frequent communication.

You've probably heard that in business, overcommunication is the enemy. Well, we changed up that dynamic and overcommunicated by design. The plan was about keeping everybody motivated, unified, and in sync.

I kicked off the communications every morning at nine o'clock with a meeting over Zoom and Facebook Live, giving everyone the to-dos and engagements for the day to prevent mind-wandering idle time and get everyone onto the same page. I didn't want our consultants in the field thinking, "Am I doing the right things? What should I be doing differently?" Sometimes, as an entrepreneur, you feel like you're out there all by yourself. But when you get on that video call and receive direction, and you see a thousand other people on that same call, it instills the tribe mentality: "I'm in business *for* myself, but I'm not *by* myself. I'm not alone. I can do this."

Then I corresponded via video calls at noon and at eight o'clock at night. These calls were about giving everyone support and assuring them they were making the right decisions. The entire time on these calls, I showed certainty and confidence—nothing wishy-washy. These women were questioning whether they could continue forward. The last thing they needed were platitudes and maybes.

I assured them all that a virtual party is just a home party in a different setting. Instead of being held in somebody's house, the party is on somebody's computer screen, but the idea remains the same. There wouldn't be face-to-face demonstrations, so now the consultants had to become more animated. They had to be more vivid and explain what the product smelled like because it couldn't be taken in through the screen. They had to become more colorful.

*Consultant Spotlight:*
## Dana Barish

*(Lives in: Annapolis, Maryland, and Jupiter, Florida; twenty years in the business)*

"This job is self-development with a paycheck, both for others and for me. I have achieved so many skills I never would have learned had I not become a Pure Romance representative. It allows me the financial freedom to travel, pay for my kids' colleges, and build the home of my dreams. It also affords me freedom, the option to do what I want when I want, and the ability to have to answer only to myself.

"My first major goal was to earn a $10,000 bonus check/commission. I remember it clearly. Someone had posted on a digital bulletin board in the company for us to state our goals. The minute I wrote it, I wished I could take it back. People were absolutely laughing at my goal. Nobody had ever gotten anywhere close to that number. Yet, there the goal sat and stared me down. So I decided, yes, that would be *my* goal.

"Once I hit that $10,000 commission goal, it was as if the floodgates opened, and now it seemed achievable to other people. So, of course I had to then stretch it and publicly state I wanted a $100,000 bonus check. Again, this seemed like me asking to buy a private island or a Learjet. However, I kept repeating the number, and soon enough everyone knew my goal. Once I hit it, it was time to set the number even higher. I can now see double and triple that amount more easily.

"The pandemic? Honestly, I could not imagine we all would have the success we are having if it weren't for Chris and his tremendous vision of what is possible in times of crisis. We all looked to his lead and ran with it, including with his daily 'Rise and Grind' Zoomcasts for the sales force. What I loved is that so many women were able to come together and share ideas so we could all succeed in a more digital space. This has made my job much easier in trying to steer our team as well.

"I always look for the good in every situation, even this one. We are now able to operate our business truly from home if we want, for one. Since we all knew that in-home parties were where all the money and success come from, it has been a pleasant surprise to see our amazing clients still wanting the Pure Romance experience but in a different way.

"Prior to Pure Romance, I was very shy when it came to adult products. I wasn't even sure a respectable household should have any. My eyes were opened after the first party I went to. People were laughing, having so much fun, and enjoying learning about the products. They weren't scary, and in fact they were just accessories to a healthy sex life in general.

"One of the things I have always loved about being a consultant is having someone come into my shopping room during a party to tell me she had no intention of buying anything. I think I probably averaged at least two of these at every party. I am not even kidding. It just goes to show you how much education is still really needed and appreciated."

We did a crash course teaching our consultants what they needed to know and do, because they didn't have the option of waiting until in-home parties came back. They had mouths to feed, people to take care of financially, and bills to pay. They had to be breadwinners *right now*.

Our daily communication also became the key to everything for our executive team in particular. Since we were no longer working in the same office, it's what kept our culture together.

Mind you, I was flying largely by the seat of my pants with most of this. We had no specific pandemic playbook. There were still plenty of days when I searched for the right answer, but I had to trust that our new plan was going to work anyway, because throwing the decisions to a committee would have led only to chaos. As a CEO, you've got to own it and you've got to live it. You've also got to communicate, first and foremost.

This is where I see so many people at the top fail. They constantly crowdsource for the right decision, to make sure everybody is happy. But in the business culture, democracies don't work all that well. One person has got to be in charge and making the decisions. You can take in a lot of input, but when push comes to shove you've got to be able to make the determinations and make them quickly on your own.

Now, some people don't like that because it's unsettling, since they've never used what God gave them—which is a great gut. Most people in charge have a bunch of analysts and a lot of data around them. I assessed things and said, "Look, we've just got to do what's right."

I decided that what made sense was being in the trenches alongside my team. I've always said that I never expect my people to do anything I wouldn't do, and as soon as I was able, I got out there working in the warehouse to keep everything moving. There were a few moments after we went into lockdown when I worried whether we would be able to get supplies to our warehouse in Loveland, Ohio, and products out to our consultants. But the supply chain wound up working out.

In the event that we got shut down entirely, I promised that we would set up distribution so our lead consultants would have their own individual inventory, like mini warehouses, and their teams could get product from them if push came to shove. That helped to reassure all the consultants.

Our whole data point, our entire structure that we discussed internally, was, "Don't worry about anything besides the customer." The customer and the consultant. That mindset was what we returned to, again and again. It was about going back to the old-school method to pin our focus on the only thing that mattered.

This pandemic has ultimately turned out to be a win for us because we've fed faith rather than fear. We went forward with optimism and took swift, decisive action. We didn't hide behind the eight ball. We didn't follow what the business community did but blazed our own trail, which is what you have to do in leadership. If you sit back and wait, nothing happens.

If you don't work your decision-making muscles, they grow flabby and weak. Those with fragile muscles find themselves unable to adapt when change comes—and in the next generation, everything is going to move at the speed of light.

For all these reasons, we became a miraculous success story during a dire time for our nation and the world. By April 2020, our business was up 89 percent. In May, it was 112 percent. And it stayed at a steady 100 percent into August despite the fact that we had shifted the entirety of what we did to an online model.

Shocking? Well, a little bit, though as I noted earlier, we always tend to do well with a bad economy, because Pure Romance is a company women turn to when they need a side hustle. But the level of our rise surprised even us.

Looking back, I can see that, besides the level of our preparation described earlier, it was really a fortunate confluence of events that worked in our favor. People were trapped at home, which meant they were having more sex and other intimate contact and were wanting to experiment more. Bedroom toys such as the ones we sell were a perfect fit.

We were also lucky that there are platforms like Zoom and Facebook out there that were so prepped to explode and serve our needs. Zoom alone ultimately saved millions of dollars for our company.

Also, as businesses closed and people were out of work and forced into the unemployment line, the number of our consultants worldwide nearly doubled—from about twenty-three thousand in January 2020 to more than forty thousand by August. Concurrently, the number of $99 introductory product kits bought soared 173 percent year over year in April and 250 percent in May. Many consultants also joined via our new $39 Social Seller Kit, which supplied new Pure Romance consultants working exclusively online with their own website and the ability to use our corporate office as a drop-ship location for product sales.

Our business essentially doubled between the spring and into the fall of 2020. It's easy to see why we upped our workforce so substantially. With well over twenty million Americans unemployed, people were thinking, "Hey, I'd better control my own destiny."

Besides teaching consultants how to plan and operate a Zoomcast or Facebook Live party, we also instructed them in the art of bundling products together for sale—for example, a toy, a lubricant, and a cleaner; or a massage oil, a massage candle, and date-night cards. Bundling took the guesswork out of product selection for the customer.

At the same time, we taught ourselves how to be a web-based business that takes the party experience from the living room to the internet. We transitioned to that completely in five weeks. This is a business that previously had done less than 10 percent of its sales online. By April of 2020, online accounted for 42 percent, and that number rose further during the spring and summer. By August, it was 55 percent.

The question gets asked, "So, does this change your business model forever?" The answer is, of course, a resounding yes. People in business school will be looking back at the pandemic as a valuable study of commerce in general. People were forced to pause their businesses, pause reality, and struggled to figure out a way to survive. Many could not. Everyone was challenged.

I'd say that 100 percent of the businesses out there are now looking at their processes, at their people, at everything they're doing, and recognizing that the pandemic has been a complete game-changer. What would typically have taken my business five years—revising our online sales structure and training our people to get them up to speed in how to make money, how to do business, and how to tell stories—we accomplished in a little more than a month, because we had no other choice. You know what they say: necessity is the mother of invention.

The COVID-19 crisis has left us with a class of consultants who will carry the torch into the new decade for us. It added a whole new arsenal to our home-party structure and set us on a course to the future.

The thing with this class of consultants is, they're a lot savvier about technology. They understand how to market on Instagram, Snapchat, and TikTok and turn followers into customers. They instinctively recognize how to tell a story online and make it translate outside the virtual world.

Those who have grown up on face-to-face selling will have a new weapon in their toolkit. They already understand customer interaction, eye contact, body language—all of that. Now, they're going to see how to address a room they aren't physically inside. We saw just how significantly the virtual business blew up in 2020 when "Zoom" became part of the vernacular as a verb.

Remember how it was beginning in March of 2020? "Let's Zoom" has become a universally understood term. It meant, "Let's get online, let's do business, let's get together, let's communicate." Zoom has opened up a whole new frontier.

One of the things we understand—and understood even when the lockdown was at its most severe—is that relationships aren't going to be canceled. Conversations aren't going to be canceled. Get-togethers aren't going to be canceled. They have just changed to a different method, a different venue, a different vehicle.

In a lot of ways, Pure Romance has provided as essential a service as supermarkets during the pandemic. People still need to eat, sleep, and, be intimate. And in terms of sexuality, our products have never been strictly for couples. If you want to have a relationship with yourself and are interested in self-discovery or self-exploration, we serve you, too. When people have a better understanding of their body, they find out what they like and don't like for those times when they're with a partner.

But for those who are part of a couple, the forced togetherness mandated by the pandemic was overall a win for intimacy products. The momentum carries on to this day.

I made a lot of intriguing discoveries myself during the pandemic about what makes me tick. I found out that I'm probably best in crisis situations, where I exercise a preternatural calm, at least outwardly. The same was true when we acquired the Slumber Parties and Passion Parties brands and workforces over the past decade. Everything that could go wrong while incorporating their people did, yet I nonetheless captained the ship confidently.

I also recall 2008, when the housing market crashed and the economy plummeted into a recession. A lot of people were saying, "Oh no, things are going out of business, Wall Street is tanking, no one's going to have any money, I need to get a second job." Pure Romance became a source of that supplementary income stream then, too.

The pandemic has also cemented my understanding that day-to-day operations aren't my strongest suit. I don't like the minutiae but love the strategy sessions. I'm not a small-picture guy but a big-picture guy. I put the right people in play and let them do their jobs. The pandemic predicament further demonstrated to me that a successful leader of an organization of any size needs to work out their decision-making muscles every single day.

The way people interact with social media has been forever changed as well. I hated Facebook. Instagram was my jam. But I flipped that during the pandemic and turned predominantly to Facebook Live, because it's where my core audience can be found. Facebook remains the number-one social platform in the world, with 2.7 billion users worldwide. I was getting hundreds of viewers on an IGTV live video broadcast but thousands on Facebook.

Here is yet another lesson I learned from the pandemic: I can still go on the road traveling for personal appearances and training sessions, but I don't need to do it two hundred-plus days a year anymore. I can put in about 50 percent of the effort for personal appearances that I used to, as long as I continue to be more active on social media and use the platforms the way they're supposed to be used.

That said, I still believe I need to carefully return to the road with strategic stops where I can build the market and promote the brand. I still crave the face-to-face connection, and I know the consultants do, too. This way, it'll be more of an event when we do come to a market. It's about taking a more strategic approach to the locations where we travel.

Every time I present at a training session makes for an exciting experience for me, because I see those who favor home parties and those who thrive to a greater extent on online sales and virtual parties coexisting beautifully. They've taught each other some valuable lessons. The crowd that favors in-home parties once said, "Forget trying to sell online. It's a waste of time. You've got to carry around your inventory and do the legwork." The online crowd came in with, "Well, I actually like the virtual parties. I'm doing really well with them, and I don't need to lug everything around."

Both sides grumble at each other a little bit, and they ultimately compromise. Maybe on Mondays and Tuesdays, instead of driving an hour each way to do a party, those in-home party lovers will turn to

Zoom. Maybe the social sellers who are new to the business will see the advantage of planning home parties strategically. Ultimately, I think we are already seeing the perfect mix of virtual and in-home.

In the end, it turns out you *can* teach old dogs new tricks, particularly when they know it's the only way for them to thrive.

Again, I'm not going to say that I am in any way pleased that the COVID-19 pandemic occurred. That would be insane and insensitive for a lot of reasons. It has been a terrible scourge on mankind, a deadly plague that has devastated hundreds of thousands of families and shattered innumerable lives economically.

Yet for many compelling reasons, the viral catastrophe has turned out to be a blessing very much in disguise for us at Pure Romance, from the standpoint of forcing our hand to change and compelling us to grow faster than we were realistically prepared to do.

Beyond that, we can genuinely say that we're not just a home-party brand anymore. We are an event-driven business for women. When it comes to building relationships with customers, we have newfound flexibility. We can do it online; we can do it at people's houses; we can do a bridal show, a bachelorette party, a VIP event, or customer appreciation. That's what has come out of this pandemic for us: a whole new tagline and an entirely new way of operating.

The answer to the question "What is Pure Romance?" now is, "We're an event-based company that sells romance and wellness products." What's more, we can do an event anywhere. Consultants can schedule an online party with somebody in Australia, somebody in New Zealand, someone in Cincinnati, someone in Los Angeles, and somebody in Puerto Rico simultaneously. They can bring together people from twenty different locations at once. It's like opening up the Wild West.

If we were offering eyeliner and mascara online, this ability wouldn't be such a big deal. But we're selling bedroom toys and lubricants. Being able to normalize and mainstream this kind of merchandise across conservative state and international borders has been huge.

But as much as I'm grateful for our company's enhanced online presence and the way we kicked virtual parties into gear, one of my most cherished lessons that COVID has taught everyone surrounds the importance of human interaction and the value of the connections we all have in our lives. Without that in-person contact, our mental health suffers greatly.

We thrive on connecting, on being around each other. When people say, "Oh sure, I connect on Facebook and Instagram," it's just not the same thing as being with people in person. There is simply no substitute for bonding and stimulating conversation in the same actual space. Having the opportunity to hug someone and give them a high five. Not a virtual hug. Not a virtual high five. The camaraderie and community we enjoy as human beings are irreplaceable.

This is not to say I'm not incredibly grateful for social media and video platforms. I am. But they are still no substitute for the real thing.

This pandemic was a giant wake-up call for humanity. It showed us as a society how much better we are together, how much we should value our relationships. When we are deprived of that human contact, we crave it more than anything.

At the end of the day, the thing of which I'm proudest when it comes to our executive and consultant teams regarding the pandemic is that they were able to face down their fears—of being bankrupt, of being infected by the virus—and persevere. As I am fond of telling them, we're born with only two fears: the fear of falling and the fear of loud noises. Everything else is just F.E.A.R. (false evidence appearing real).

My obligation to spearhead and lead this organization during the pandemic ultimately was greater than my anxiety over what might be coming next.

Meanwhile, the year(s) ahead will find us in a whole new ballgame. We plan to be in Cincinnati for our National Training in August 2021, rolling out products we hope to launch and starting a whole new conversation about sexual wellness. We intend in the near term to find our stride in rebranding how Pure Romance operates in this new world that combines home parties and the online sphere.

We have to constantly be working on our brand and on ourselves. You can't stay with the status quo or you're asking for trouble. It took a global health emergency to teach us just how imperative it is to continually be striving to improve.

I see home parties coming back stronger than ever going forward. People will have dinner parties. They'll socialize. They'll gather with friends and family. Things may not return entirely to normal for a little while. But we are ultimately going to be okay.

To close out this chapter, here is a mini Q&A I did with my mom addressing the pandemic.

**Chris Cicchinelli:** How did the pandemic change your view of how this business can work?

**Patty Brisben:** It shows you how incredibly resilient women can be in business. I remember when the whole thing broke and we began to lock down in March '20. You and I met in a restaurant that was practically deserted, and we agreed that we basically had to build and reinforce our e-commerce component overnight, that we had to restructure a company known for home parties of luxury items. And I saw you turn that around very quickly.

**CC:** How do you think we were able to do that?

**PB:** Well, nobody seemed to be in panic mode, even though I knew you and the executive team had to be feeling that. You steered the consultants to 100 percent virtual parties in what seemed like a couple of weeks.

**CC:** What do you think the fallout from COVID-19 will be for Pure Romance over the next few years?

**PB:** I don't think things will go back to being the way they were for a while, if ever. Our women see just how significantly virtual parties and online sales can impact their totals.

**CC:** So, what's the lesson you think we take away from this?

**PB:** I think what we witnessed with the pandemic was the pushing of a reset button. It was horrible. A lot of people have lost their lives and livelihoods. But we as a company were extremely fortunate, in part because we smartly pivoted. With Zoom and Facebook Live and building those virtual relationships, it is officially a substantial adjunct to our repertoire that is here to stay and grow.

I'd just like to conclude here that the irony of all of this having happened in the year 2020 isn't lost on me. We came out of it with people really being able to clearly see what's important in their businesses and their lives. To some degree, none of us will ever be the same again—for better and for worse.

## Takeaways

- Leadership is about you stepping up. You have to be the strongest voice, the one with a plan. You have to remember that where some people have struggles, others find opportunities. Every challenge is a new chance to discover something profound about yourself and shine a light for others to follow, even during the darkest of times like we experienced in 2020 and into 2021.

- Particularly in the middle of a crisis situation, communicating fast and often is key. I never show up to lose. I'm a hard hitter. Sometimes, I hit too hard and have to take a step back. But I will always err on the side of pushing a little too much in the interest of motivation. To my mind, that's what being a leader is all about.

- Your decision-making muscle is like any other muscle. The more you use it, the better shape it will be in. This is why, as a business owner, you have to step up and never be afraid to make the decision. Your business isn't a democracy. You can and should crowdsource to tap the hive mind, as we did when COVID happened in quickly creating a pandemic task force. But you ultimately have to be in charge, make the final decision, and own it.

# CHAPTER 12

# Now It's Up to You

My hope is that this book has supplied a road map for those of you considering not only a career as a Pure Romance consultant or in sales but a career of any sort. My goal was to impart sound advice that can help generate success at every point of your career journey.

Try not to fret if you're feeling at a dead end. Heck, the worldwide pandemic has significantly impacted all of us. Cut yourself some slack. The bottom line is, no matter your age or your stage, there's always time to turn your ship around and head to a new port or bring renewed focus to your current work life. You simply have to imagine you can do it, stay positive, and sell yourself using the tips I've just provided you.

I'm here to tell you that there is nothing standing between you and your dreams except you. Turning your aspirations into reality is all about believing they can happen—because they can.

You have the power within you to become the person you've always desired to be. I've seen it happen time and time again. You focus on a goal and accept nothing less than to achieve it. You harness the energy and, in tandem with what I've taught you in the preceding pages, you move steadfastly toward making it all happen.

It's really a pretty powerful concept when you think about it. Nothing can stop you except you. You're the one who is in charge. If you summon the proper strength and focus, there is literally nothing that you can't achieve. Again, use the example of me, someone who graduated near the bottom of his class with a reading disability yet through hard work was able to achieve all of his goals. There is not a reason in the world this can't be you, too.

However, I caution to remind you that this isn't going to be easy. If it were, everyone would be wealthy and successful. It's a grind. It isn't all rainbows and unicorns. There will be days when you curse the fates and wonder, "Why can't this be easier?" There will be days when you ask, "What am I doing wrong?" There will be days when it feels like success is so elusive that it's never going to happen. Those are the times when you need to grasp your internal remote and set it to the big picture.

Take a lot of deep breaths. Take a lot of stock. Don't get sidetracked by things that don't matter. There will be plenty of disappointments along the way, but you need to move past them and take the long view. This thing is a marathon, never a sprint. And remember, you are a warrior! You are the wind beneath your wings! You are the one who can make it all happen, because you will accept nothing less.

One thing that people who succeed in business and in life all have in common is persistence. When they get knocked down, they don't stay there. They get up, dust themselves off, and get back in the ring. That really is the key difference between those who make it and those who don't. The successful ones don't give up when that first arrow pierces their armor. The ones who keep moving forward don't look at their failures as serious wounds but mere stumbles on the way to the goal line. Throwing in the towel simply is not an option.

With that in mind, here once again are some of the most important lessons I've imparted in this book, for handy reference—because, you know, repetition always wins the day.

- **Live your life by design, not default:** Always remember that *you* are the architect of design for your life and business. You are not following a blueprint drawn up by anyone else—not your peers, not your coworkers, not your boss, no one. We design our bedroom, our kitchen, and our bathroom. Our life should be the same way. Think of it like Pinterest. Design the life *you* want.

- **Luck is preparation meeting opportunity:** I think it's insulting to dismiss someone's success strictly as a matter of luck. It's never luck. I mean, luck doesn't hurt, but you need to be ready when luck comes calling. That's where you come in.

- **Get comfortable with being uncomfortable:** This means that you should come to terms with always being hungry and never feeling completely satisfied. The uncomfortable ones are consistently striving, always wanting more. This is where you want to be. You have to want it more than the other person.

- **The most important things people bring to the job every day are their attitude and their motivation:** Your attitude is literally 100 percent of what drives your success. Your motivation is in fact tied entirely into your attitude. The two are linked. You can't have one without the other.

- **If you want to be successful in business, you need to put yourself out there and do the grind:** What this alludes to is the fact nothing is going to be easy, and you need to embrace that and welcome the burn. If it feels like it's too easy, that means you aren't putting out maximum effort.

- **Play the ball; don't let the ball play you:** It's about being proactive, not reactive. Stay in control and the world is yours. Allow yourself to be controlled and you're never able to meet your full potential. It's that simple.

- **You always want to be in front of the change, never behind it:** Meet the moment by dictating it with your actions. That cements your status as a front-runner rather than someone who is always struggling to catch up.

- **Everything in business is about the willingness and ability to evolve:** You can't stay in the same spot. Making it to the next level is always a matter of moving to the next level. But to do it effectively, you need to be open to the idea that your evolution is necessary in the first place.

- **To succeed in life and in business and sell yourself to the world, always be grateful for the things you *have* rather than pining for the things you *want*:** Being grateful for your blessings is the secret not only to success but happiness. Gratitude is the best attitude in all things.

- **Typically, nothing worth achieving happens overnight:** As I repeatedly stressed earlier, this may be the most important lesson you'll learn. If you want to accomplish something long-lasting, you need to exercise patience (not my strongest suit) and determination. And stay the course. The rewards will come.

- **Your most valuable currency isn't money but choice:** This is something I discovered after being fortunate enough to become involved in a business on the rise. It's not the money but the options and possibilities that money brings you that matter the most. That's what being truly wealthy is all about.

- **Commit to the process, detach from the outcome:** Put all of yourself into the process and then remove yourself from the result. It's where you *really* need to practice patience, because too often we focus almost exclusively on how long it's going to take to get to the end goal rather than the value of the steps required to achieve it.

- **Anything worth doing is worth doing well:** Don't ever just mail it in. Be resourceful and work your butt off and put every ounce of you into everything you do, because every meeting you take, every sale you make, and every call and email you put out there represents you and your brand. Maximum effort makes all the difference.

- **You're never going to please anybody if you concentrate on trying to please everybody:** This is an axiom that has rung true forever. By attempting to please everyone, no one will wind up happy. So, make sure instead to please yourself by always doing the right thing. Also, never compromise yourself or your integrity to make a sale or get the job.

- **Be stronger than your strongest excuse:** We all do it. The weather was awful. The traffic was insane. Some issue prevented us from doing what we needed to do. Now is the time for you to get past all that and declare, "I am the controller of my destiny." It's you who's in charge, not fate.

- **You can change the world at any age:** Mozart wrote his first symphony at the age of five. Nadia Comăneci was an Olympic champion at fourteen. Sara Blakely was only twenty-seven when she founded Spanx. On the other side of the ledger, Sam Walton was forty-four when he opened his first Walmart, while J. R. R. Tolkien was sixty-two when he published *The Lord of the Rings*. Age is never an excuse. No matter how old or young you are, you've got this.

- **You have to be the one in the room who controls the narrative:** This is about not leaving anything to chance, including presuming that everyone else (or *anyone* else) in the room knows what they're doing. You are the only one you can count on to make things happen and move the needle.

- **Life is not a dress rehearsal:** You already know this, of course, but it never hurts to have a reminder. This isn't a dress rehearsal but the real deal. There are no second chances at this, so far as we know, so let's do it right the first time. Be mindful of this every day.

- **Do the right thing, and you'll never have to worry that you didn't:** I don't care who you are, you know what the right thing is. Honesty, integrity, fairness, decency—they all matter in everything you do. Being a good person is nonnegotiable because it makes all the other things possible. It also keeps your conscience clear.

- **The playing field is never level. It's skewed to benefit those who work harder and smarter and have a better product:** There is no fairness in your business life. Eliminate that from your list of expectations. You have to win consumers over by being better than your competitor. That's just Business 101, but you would be surprised how many people are thrown off by this basic idea.

- **You are your number-one asset:** The one person—the *only* person—you can always count on is you. You must be the center of your universe. This doesn't mean that you don't take others' feelings and needs into consideration, just that you must protect your brand and your reputation at all costs.

- **Your work ethic is something you have to instill in yourself:** You wouldn't believe how many smart and talented people I've seen who didn't have the go-getter instinct that makes all the difference between success and failure. It isn't something you're born with. You need to cultivate it from deep inside. Once you dig down to tap that will, nothing can stop you.

- **You have to believe you have the gift inside of you, and your job is to get it out and share it with the world—because the world is waiting:** It's incredibly important to believe that you're someone special, because if you don't think you're amazing, chances are no one else will, either. Even if you have to talk yourself into it, have that talk. Once you do, that's when the magic happens. The world needs what you bring to the table. Never doubt that.

- **You have the power to change your mindset and your circumstances:** There have been times when you feel stuck in a rut. We all suffer from it on occasion. But it doesn't have to become a chronic condition, because you have the power to change up the narrative. Give yourself permission to alter your situation and a whole world of possibilities will become clear.

- **"Repetition is the mother of learning and the father of action, which makes it the architect of accomplishment." —Zig Ziglar:** This is such a great quote, and so true, that I based an entire chapter on it. It's also something I believe with all my heart and soul. Repeat things until they become habit and you'll be on the road to doing life better.

- **Frequency breeds familiarity. Familiarity ultimately becomes trust. Trust is what spurs buying:** We've already established that people don't buy products; they buy people. This is why your clients need to get to know you beyond the sale. Once you become a regular part of their routine, trust grows. Trust is where the secret of all success resides.

- **Good is the enemy of great:** Doing things in a way that's good enough is easy. It's so easy that too many of us settle for it when making what we do great requires just a little bit more effort. Never allow yourself to fall into the "good enough" trap. The road of failure is littered with those who thought "good" was going to cut it. It won't. You need to be exceptional, and exceptional requires you to put everything you've got into it.

- **If you don't work your decision-making muscles, they grow flabby and weak:** The muscles that make decisions are like any other muscles in the human body. When you work and tone them, they spring to life and become stronger. When you fail to put that effort into them, they atrophy. Keep your decision muscles toned and they'll be there, ready when you need them.

- **Where some people have struggles, others find opportunities:** There are those out there whom we avoid. Do you know why? Because they constantly pepper us with an endless stream of complaints. The reason they consistently fail is that everything goes wrong for them, and it's never their fault. Fate simply frowns on them. Yet there are others who meet their frustrations by turning them into opportunities to thrive in a different way. Those are the people who become legends.

- **We can't control our conditions. We can control only our choices:** Things are going to go wrong. I like to say that 15 percent of my plans are going to go south because of the nature of life. There are going to be rainstorms in your business, and your job should be to meet those disappointments with optimism and resolve. You can choose to gripe or to say, "I'm going to overcome this."

Your choice to pick up this book was a great one. The business guidelines provided here are the first step on your path to maximizing success not just in your work life but your personal life, too. Take what you've read here to heart and you'll be on your way to a whole new level of achievement and fulfillment.

The secret, after all, is you.

# How They Did It:
# Pure Romance Success Stories

The way I see it, my job is to teach our consultants how to build their brand and operate their own independent business. As soon as they make the consultant commitment—whether it be Pure Romance by Dana or Pure Romance by Heather—they are representing not only the company but themselves.

How you treat a waitress, a hotel worker, a customer, or anyone else out in public is super important, because in these days of social media when everyone's carrying around a mini video camera in their pocket, you're always on. There are so many ways to be visible, scrutinized, and recorded that you're never really off the clock in terms of how you conduct yourself. How you behave, how you appear, the way you demonstrate your work ethic—all are intrinsically linked to your brand.

Some women learned early on the value of that brand and transformed themselves into Pure Romance superstars. I'm thinking of five of them in particular: Janna Vukelich, Cindy Faulkner, Nikki Hughes, Angelia Robinson, and Ashley Livermore.

All five in this quintet originally got involved with the company as a side gig, only to see it blossom into their primary and a six-figure annual income. Their secret? They dedicated themselves, lived their lives by design and not default, and committed to the process while detaching from the outcome. They also were prepared to effectively pivot when the COVID-19 pandemic reared its ugly head.

It didn't hurt that they also listened well. Not that I'm going to take any of the credit, since the secret is *them*. But each of their stories is inspirational, instructive, and unique, as you'll see in the following Q&As.

### Janna Vukelich

*Age forty-four, senior executive director and executive board of directors member at Pure Romance; Apple Valley, Minnesota*

*Janna Vukelich had a stressful career as a government lobbyist and was looking to transition out when her mother became ill and she was tasked with taking care of her. She was looking around for an alternative career when Pure Romance entered her life. The rest is history.*

**Chris Cicchinelli:** Let's start off by asking how you got involved in Pure Romance.

**Janna Vukelich:** It was 2007. I had just turned thirty and was working as a lobbyist in the nonprofit sector. I knew I wanted to transition out of it, because the pay certainly wasn't great, it was really stressful, and the hours were long. I also had a terrible public speaking anxiety, which is especially difficult because I had to testify at the Minnesota State Capitol fairly regularly. But it was too early for me to have a midlife crisis. I heard about Pure Romance and thought it might be a fun thing to try that was completely out of my comfort zone, kind of a personal development project to see if I could work through my speaking phobia while figuring out my next career move. Plus, I'd always wanted to own a business, but it seemed like this big, overwhelming thing. I imagined this would help hone my business management skills.

**CC:** Was your working with Pure Romance initially any sort of issue with your friends or family, coworkers, or spouse or significant other?

**JV:** There were and are people who shut down immediately when they find out what you do. But for me personally, it's never been an issue. I have always been someone who likes to go against the grain. So I've actually enjoyed that part of it. I look sweet and I sound sweet, but I've always had a bit of the rebel inside me. No one was going to tell me that a job I loved didn't meet their idea of acceptable. So if they didn't like what I was doing, you know, bring it on.

**CC:** How long did it take for you to get into a groove with selling and positively impact your financial life?

**JV:** It was maybe one party a month for the first five months. I was just dipping my toes in to see what it was all about. Then, once the legislative session ended in Minnesota, I ramped it up. I made about $15,000 that first year. There's a learning curve, and if you can get through the first year—which is always rough, because you're constantly pounding the pavement and building up your client base—you get way better at it. A little over a year after I started, I left the other job, and this became my primary gig. My income rose steadily after that.

**CC:** What has been the most challenging part of running your own Pure Romance business?

**JV:** For me, the toughest thing has been getting outside my comfort zone and motivating myself while not having someone looking over my shoulder. I've had to personally instill the kind of discipline that doesn't come easily for me. I'm also a natural introvert, so I have to stay on myself to be outgoing and push that part of me.

**CC:** What has been the greatest thing about operating your own business? Is it the independence? The money? The ability to enhance people's intimate relationships? All of the above?

**JV:** It's definitely all of those things, but for me, it's mostly just the freedom to do what I want, when I want, with whom I want. To be my own boss, have fun, and make money. To not have someone always breathing down my neck to perform. Running things on my own terms and at my own pace. Also, knowing that I'm making a positive impact is incredibly important. It's the whole shebang.

**CC:** What stigma do you personally find is still attached to selling our products? How have you seen it change?

**JV:** I think there still is definitely a stigma. Women deserve to have conversations about their bodies that are respectful, that are candid, that are fun, and there remain a lot of barriers to that happening. But I feel like it's gotten easier. People are more open at a younger age to discuss it candidly, and I think it's often better received with gals who are in their early twenties than those in my own age group. I personally like the fact that our company is on a mission to break down those barriers. I frankly sometimes wish it were considered a greater taboo than it is! But your mother worked very hard to devulgarize this industry, and it's mostly worked.

**CC:** Can you share your income trajectory from Pure Romance and how it has remained consistent or risen over the years?

**JV:** I'm not one of the top sellers in the company, but I average about $75,000 a year or so. I'm going to guess that I've sold, since I started, probably close to $900,000 worth of product. A lot of what I earn comes from my team. Much of what I see comes out of my motivating them. This one girl on my team was working at a bakery, has five kids, and we did a virtual party collaboratively where she sold $500 worth of products. So it's a nice opportunity for people who are just looking for a little bit of supplemental income.

**CC:** How tough was it for you and your team to adjust to the COVID-19 pandemic?

**JV:** In terms of my personal business, there wasn't as big a shift, because that happened after my son was born and my husband started traveling a lot several years back, when I decided to transition things mostly online. The only time I was worried came when it looked like our warehouse might shut down for a minute after Ohio had the stay-at-home order, and I worried that we might not have product to move. Instead, the opposite happened, and our team sales rose sharply. We also had more than two hundred new consultants join our team over a couple of months.

**CC:** In what ways do you think our company has been changed by the pandemic?

**JV:** Especially for our gals who might be a little more on the introverted side like me, it opened up their eyes that you can really do this business multiple ways. You don't have to be the home-party-girl extraordinaire to make this work. We've cracked things open in terms of the range of possibilities, virtual as well as in-home. I don't think things are ever going to be the same as they were, and that's good. Our business had been so weighted within home parties before, but now we can offer the best of both worlds. It's already expanding things in such a cool way.

**CC:** Finally, I'm looking for some honest feedback on how you see my leadership.

**JV:** The truth is that you are an incredible leader. You lead by example. You're right out there in the trenches with us. You walk the walk. When I've been on the road with you, I see you putting together gift boxes for people. You ride along with the staff for our events. You never play the prima donna. But at the same time, you aren't afraid to pivot. You're not afraid of change. You know we have to evolve or become extinct. After the pandemic hit, you filled out our website within a matter of days to make it more conducive to e-commerce. With a different leader, this could all have gone south in a hurry.

### Cindy Faulkner

*Age forty-nine, executive director and executive board of directors member at Pure Romance; Chattanooga, Tennessee*

*Pure and simple, Cindy Faulkner is a Pure Romance legend. She leads an amazing team out of Tennessee. When she joined the company at age thirty-one, Cindy was, in her own words, "desperate and broken in so many ways." As a member of a Baptist family, she had endured a lot of shame around the word "sex" but still yearned to know and intimately understand her body. Once she did, she looked to pass on her knowledge to others.*

**Chris Cicchinelli:** Let's start off by asking how you got involved in Pure Romance.

**Cindy Faulkner:** It happened for me back in 2003. I was working as a nurse and had no interest at all in direct sales when Pure Romance came into my life. I was trapped in a bad marriage and about to file for divorce. This was part of changing up who I was, who I had been. At the time, I'd never had an orgasm and didn't know where my clitoris was. Even saying the word "clitoris" was hard, and I'd been to nursing school. That part of my body simply wasn't functioning—or so I thought. But anyway, I got into this originally as a part-time thing. It turned into a passion and a mission, and ultimately my calling, to be able to impact and influence women about their sexual health and personal growth.

**CC:** Was your working with Pure Romance initially any sort of issue with your friends or family, coworkers, or spouse or significant other?

**CF:** Well, I do live in the backwoods of Tennessee. My whole immediate and extended family is in the ministry, so you can imagine what they thought of my being involved in this business. Self-pleasure was a no-no. Sex in general had a negative connotation. There was a lot of shame surrounding it, and that obviously worked on my head. I got a divorce and was selling sex toys three months later. I'm sure most members of my family were thinking, "It's so sad. Poor Cindy has lost her mind." But I never settled for their assessment and reasoning. Going in, even as I put one foot in front of the other, I was scared to death. But the day I started, I chose faith over fear, which was a big deal for me as a people pleaser.

**CC:** How long did it take for you to get into a groove with selling and positively impact your financial life?

**CF:** My older sister, who was pretty much the only person in my family who supported me, hosted my first party. I booked five parties off that one, so that helped me to create some momentum pretty quickly. I didn't do anything special, really, but I was consistent. I worked it. I don't think I realized how emotionally deficient and depleted I was until I started enjoying myself as a consultant. After a year, I made the board of directors. After a little over two years, I was able to quit nursing and do this full time.

**CC:** What has been the most challenging part of running your own Pure Romance business?

**CF:** The consistently toughest thing for me is self-leadership, because I can't lead others if I don't lead myself well. And I can't expect from others what I'm not willing to do for myself. When unfortunate things or painful things happen, owning my part in it has been a real challenge and the hardest thing. During those times when I've been able to handle that well, it's created huge success in my business.

**CC:** What has been the greatest thing about operating your own business? Is it the independence? The money? The ability to enhance people's intimate relationships? All of the above?

**CF:** It's the independent choices that I have. I love the word "choices." This job gives me time choice, money choice, the choice of with whom and how I choose to spend my life because of the flexibility it affords me. It's also the impact and influence that I've been blessed with, along with the honor to have the women who are in my life, whether it's clients, my team of consultants in general, or my friends.

**CC:** What stigma do you personally find is still attached to selling our products? How have you seen it change?

**CF:** "Permission" is my big word. I gave myself permission to overcome my own psychological issues surrounding my body, and at the same time permission to look past the stigma. The stigma is still there for sure—I mean, I'm in the Bible Belt—but there is no place I'd rather be. I've helped to decrease the stigma in my area and feel pride in having opened up a conversation for women with both themselves and their significant others. That's something I could never have imagined happening at the start of my tenure.

**CC:** Can you share your income trajectory from Pure Romance and how it has remained consistent or risen over the years?

**CF:** What I earn has gone up steadily nearly every year. For my first seventeen years doing this, I think I personally sold probably $1.5 million worth of products while spearheading a $3 million-plus annual team. In terms of the most I've ever earned in a year, I'd say gross would be about $250,000. I average well into six figures.

**CC:** How tough was it for you and your team to adjust to the COVID-19 pandemic?

**CF:** Well, I admit that I was kind of petrified at first; I'm not going to lie. I'm not like these millennials who do social media and online so smoothly. It takes me a little while to navigate and figure it out. There were a couple of days where I was kind of frozen. I allowed myself to feel the uncertainty, the helplessness, the powerlessness, but then I adjusted to the process and moved past it. I canceled all my in-home parties and turned them into Zoom virtual parties. I got in my mojo and figured it out, small steps, moving forward one day at a time, encouraging my team. If I didn't get the result I wanted, I tweaked it.

**CC:** In what ways do you think our company has been changed by the pandemic?

**CF:** You know, as I told my friends, it was really like starting an entirely new business in many ways. That goes both for me personally and for Pure Romance as a whole. I don't see things going entirely back to the way they were, with in-home dominating. I believe we'll be able to have a nice, beautiful little rhythm between in-home and online. I see it appealing to even more consultants and being able to sponsor more of them, so it's truly going to work as a blessing in disguise.

**CC:** Finally, I'm looking for some honest feedback on how you see my leadership.

**CF:** Well, the tears are going to come now. You have been such a big part of my journey. You remember that at one point I traveled with you on the road for five or six years straight, and you were like my brother. Your leadership and willingness to speak to us consultants in the field are tremendous. You are caring, first and foremost. And because you care, we listen. Plus, you're always twenty steps ahead of everyone else. I haven't always liked every decision you've made, but I know you're protecting our future.

## Nikki Hughes

*Age forty-one, senior executive director and executive board of directors member at Pure Romance; New Baltimore, Michigan*

*Nikki Hughes was a single mother looking for a way to fund her car payment and a backup plan to provide for her family in case of a layoff at the Ford plant in Michigan where she still works. Little did she know that her true purpose would soon come from an unlikely place.*

**Chris Cicchinelli:** Let's start off by asking how you got involved in Pure Romance.

**Nikki Hughes:** In 2008, I was building trucks on the Ford Motor assembly line here in Michigan, which I've done now for over twenty years. I was just looking to make some extra money with a second job. Never had any intention of quitting Ford, and I haven't quit. For five years prior to my signing up, I'd attended Pure Romance parties thrown by my girlfriends. I had gone through a divorce. I was a single mom with two small kids, and I thought, "You know, I deserve to have some wine, some fun, and a little girl time." I hosted a few parties. But whenever I was asked if I would like to be a consultant, I thought, "Absolutely not." Then I finally decided to take a chance and never looked back.

**CC:** Was your working with Pure Romance initially any sort of issue with your friends or family, coworkers, or spouse or significant other?

**NH:** I was already involved in this before I met my current husband. But it was rarely an issue with my other family members. I did hear from a few who would say, "That's a pyramid scheme. Why are you wasting your time?" But then I wound up making more money than the person who signed me up, for four years in a row. So much for any scheme. The trickiest part was probably when I would see women from my church at my parties. I would be like, "Wait a second, I know you." But usually the response was, "What you're doing is really cool."

**CC:** How long did it take for you to get into a groove with selling and positively impact your financial life?

**NH:** My first year, I did $7,000 in sales. It started out that Ford was my Plan A and this was my Plan B, but that flipped a couple of years after I started. I got it up into six figures annually a long time ago. But my strong suit turned out to be sponsoring. The way I look at it, one conversation can pay me for months on end. I learned early on that mentoring and teaching are the way to be most effective in this business.

**CC:** What has been the most challenging part of running your own Pure Romance business?

**NH:** I think the most challenging part is just change and fear of the unknown, like with the COVID-19 pandemic. Also, I'm going to say time management. Until the COVID thing happened, I was doing six to eight in-home parties a month. Combined with Ford, the two jobs make for a big work commitment, especially since my husband and I have four kids with a blended family. But the party planning doesn't feel like it's too much, because honestly, to me, Pure Romance is a lifestyle. It's who I am. Everyone in my family knows what a priority this is for me.

**CC:** What has been the greatest thing about operating your own business? Is it the independence? The money? The ability to enhance people's intimate relationships? All of the above?

**NH:** My favorite thing is that this business is mine and mine alone. Nobody can do it for me, and nobody can take it away. I love the fact that what I've built is all based on grit and hard work and focus and belief and self-reliance. It's really cool when I can tell the ladies on my team, "This is yours." I hire a lot of girls who are newly divorced or young moms, or college students, or women who are just trying to regain their equilibrium and reacquaint themselves with who they are. That's what is so rewarding.

**CC:** What stigma do you personally find is still attached to selling our products? How have you seen it change?

**NH:** I've always had quite a strong faith, and I was raised in a very religious household. That faith continues to this day. My husband and I are both involved with our church—the Rock Church, which is non-denominational—and our worship team. The stigma of what I do is still there to some degree. I know I get some people talking behind my back at Ford, which can be a harsh culture. But I'm so passionate about helping women and their relationships that it kind of fell by the wayside, because I feel like what I'm doing is more powerful than any stigma.

**CC:** Can you share your income trajectory from Pure Romance and how it has remained consistent or risen over the years?

**NH:** The only year that I didn't sell $90,000 to $100,000 worth of product was my first one. My high was $122,000, in 2019. But the thing that's most important is what our team collectively sells, and in 2019 that was $3.2 million. I'm sure it will be even higher in 2020.

**CC:** How tough was it for you and your team to adjust to the COVID-19 pandemic?

**NH:** By springtime of 2020 in the midst of COVID-19, our consultant team numbers just soared. We had risen from about three hundred-something to six hundred by April, adding more than two hundred consultants in just thirty days. I was up 64 percent in my own business, year over year. Crazy, right? But despite that, I battled to get the hang of the virtual parties. I'm a social butterfly. I love being in a house and doing product demonstrations. I pivoted nearly overnight from in-home to virtual, but being a hands-on person, sitting behind a screen was tough. At the same time, I had to dive into the pool first and show my team the way, even while I was craving human contact and just wanting to hug someone.

**CC:** In what ways do you think our company has been changed by the pandemic?

**NH:** This business is all about change. Our products change, so it makes sense that the way we sell them should change, too. But my opinion is, we're going to see a big return to in-home parties going forward, even if there is initially some distancing involved. People need that human connection, and we're just going to blow things straight out of the water, increasingly as time goes on. Will virtual parties always be part of the mix now? Definitely. But you can only get so much through the screen. People are going to appreciate their relationships and that one-on-one contact even more, in a way that will improve business overall.

**CC:** Finally, I'm looking for some honest feedback on how you see my leadership.

**NH:** You can steer my ship anywhere. That's the absolute truth. You've never done me wrong or let the consultants down in nearly twelve years. You could say, "Okay, we're going to walk through these hot coals. Here's how it's going to feel; are you ready?" and I would say, "Ready when you are." You believed in me before I believed in myself. You pivoted us expertly during COVID. I don't know anyone else who could have made that happen so quickly, seamlessly, and effectively.

## Angelia (pronounced "AN-juh-lic") Robinson

*Age forty-eight, senior executive director and board of directors member at Pure Romance; Fort Worth, Texas*

*Angelia Robinson was falling into a depression. She hated her work life and was stressing over how she was going to change her story. At forty-two years old, she was newly divorced, living paycheck to paycheck, and had just been evicted from her home. She was in a new state with no family or friends and had nowhere to turn. Plus, she had a newborn. Then came Pure Romance.*

**Chris Cicchinelli:** Let's start off by asking how you got involved in Pure Romance.

**Angelia Robinson:** I worked as a recording artist for many years but had to retire from performing and was just coming out of a sixteen-year marriage, fourteen of which were unhappy. I had recently moved from Maryland to Texas, had my fifth child, and been working for two years at a call center doing telemarketing. This was now 2015. I happened to be on Instagram one day when I saw that Dana Barish—who used to be my fitness instructor—was doing incredibly well selling these products for Pure Romance. I reached out to her to find out what it was all about. I'd never even been to one of these parties, but she imparted the belief that it was real and I could be successful doing it, too.

**CC:** Was your working with Pure Romance initially any sort of issue with your friends or family, coworkers, or spouse or significant other?

**AR:** The only pushback came from my mother. She would tell people, "Oh my God, now Angelia is selling sex toys! What is she doing?" But I was having a conversation with her one day where she was sharing some of the intimate details of her life, and I said, "Mom, don't you know this is what I teach women about every day?" She allowed me to educate her and wound up saying, "Wow, if I'd have known all this stuff, I'd have gotten a vibrator long ago." Surprisingly, despite coming from the very judgmental gospel and Christian music industry, I never got any backlash from them.

**CC:** How long did it take for you to get into a groove with selling and positively impact your financial life?

**AR:** So, I got this sales kit and didn't know what to do with it. I went to shadow a girl at one of her parties. I was really nervous, having no idea at all what to expect. But I had a blast. It was like girls' night. Things really changed for me after I went to the Pure Romance World Conference in March 2016. I saw all of these women taking home awards and being honored, and I said to myself, "I'm going to really figure this thing out and walk that stage next year." And I did. I got myself fired from my call center job on purpose so I could do this full time, and I made six figures and became a senior executive director within two years.

**CC:** What has been the most challenging part of running your own Pure Romance business?

**AR:** The big challenge for me is learning the work-life balance. I was just up all night after doing a virtual mega-party last night. I literally didn't sleep, because I'm a resolution junkie. I had to go through all my order forms and send out follow-up messages to everybody. I like to strike while the iron is hot and reach out to my team to give them follow-up information. I love what I do and live, eat, sleep, and breathe this. So, avoiding becoming a workaholic and being present when I'm with my family, that's the hardest thing for me.

**CC:** What has been the greatest thing about operating your own business? Is it the independence? The money? The ability to enhance people's intimate relationships? All of the above?

**AR:** All of the above. For somebody like me who gets bored very easily, this job has been a revelation. In my past jobs, I would just show up for work and do things halfway. That's impossible for me at Pure Romance. You can't get bored. There are always new products. There are always new people. You can always change a party up and do a new game. I needed something that I couldn't get bored with, and it took until I was in my forties to find it, but I did.

**CC:** What stigma do you personally find is still attached to selling our products? How have you seen it change?

**AR:** Stigma has never been an issue. For me, there might have been instead a little concern that, being a minority myself, most of my parties were with minority women who didn't have the education in sex and sexual health. So, whereas they might spend $200 on a pair of Jordans or $600 on a designer handbag, they weren't going to fork over $200 on a toy, because they didn't see the value in it. But as you told me in my first Future Leader class, "It's not about race. It's about education." That has turned out to be true. For my Black, brown, and Asian clients, I'm educating, and they're growing with me.

**CC:** Can you share your income trajectory from Pure Romance and how it has remained consistent or risen over the years?

**AR:** I've been doing this only six years now, and I hit six figures in my third year. It went up a little bit in 2018 and 2019 and then a lot in 2020, during the pandemic, when we were all shocked to see the level of our growth. But quite honestly, my focus is on my team and building leaders, as you teach us, rather than on my personal income growth.

**CC:** How tough was it for you and your team to adjust to the COVID-19 pandemic?

**AR:** None of us had any idea what the pandemic was going to mean to our business. We were all a little shaken up at first. It was rough having to shift away from in-home parties, then our team saw something like 250-plus percent growth throughout the springtime of 2020 and into the summer. But to be honest, you are such a phenomenal businessman and such a great coach that I was never once fearful that things weren't going to go our way. That's the truth. You were like, "Just in case we get shut down, I'm going to set things up so you guys have mini warehouses, so you have inventory." That was very reassuring.

**CC:** In what ways do you think our company has been changed by the pandemic?

**AR:** I think that it's opened things up for us. What we learned during COVID ultimately gives us more opportunity and more reach. For example, I was able to do a virtual party in 2020 with these sorority sisters in Bermuda. It was perfect for them. They had not seen each other in a long time, and they all managed to be in their own bedrooms or living rooms sipping a cocktail and ordering products over Zoom. I feel like we as a company are coming out of this better than if it had never happened in the first place. It helps that I'm the kind of person who jumps off the cliff and figures out how I'm going to land on the way down.

**CC:** Finally, I'm looking for some honest feedback on how you see my leadership.

**AR:** You know what I love about you? Your honesty and integrity. I just remember what you told us when everything was starting to roll during the pandemic. You said, "Listen, ride this wave while you can, because things are going to level off. We know everybody's making crazy money now, but don't spend it. Put it away, because this isn't going to last forever." I've met a lot of great leaders in the church as well as outside the church, in business, all over. But no one has ever drawn me to them like you have. You're just an authentic leader. I love the way you have our backs and take care of the team like we're your family. You have helped me to get my life in order financially and every which way. You've been a blessing. Sorry, that's just the reality.

## Ashley Livermore

*Age thirty-eight, senior executive director and senior board of directors member at Pure Romance; South Mills, North Carolina*

*When she started at Pure Romance, Ashley Livermore was a broke teacher with no savings account and a huge amount of student loan debt that couldn't be paid on just her teacher's salary. She lacked confidence and was worried that no matter what she did in her career, it was never going to get her out of the trailer park where she was living.*

**Chris Cicchinelli:** Let's start off by asking how you got involved in Pure Romance.

**Ashley Livermore:** In 2007, I had been teaching fifth grade for six years, living in a very small town in North Carolina and taking home about $1,800 a month, $750 of which was going to pay off my student loans. I was looking for something I could do as a part-time thing that I could make work with my teacher schedule. My sister was interested in doing Pure Romance herself and turned me on to the idea. She ultimately decided against it, but meanwhile, I went to the website, was intrigued, and signed up. It wasn't all peaches and cream from there, but I was determined to make it work. With those loans hanging over my head, I didn't have a whole lot of choice. I had to have a second job.

**CC:** Was your working with Pure Romance initially any sort of issue with your friends or family, coworkers, or spouse or significant other?

**AL:** I was engaged when I originally got involved, and my fiancé came home one day to find these two big boxes on the porch. He comes up to me and asks, "What are you doing?" I explained that I'd signed up for Pure Romance, that I didn't earn enough as a teacher for us to make ends meet, and we lived in a trailer park. He said, "So you're going to be a 'ding slinger,'" which is slang for someone who sells "ding-a-lings." I told him, "No, I'm going to prove you wrong." I earned a $300 profit from my first party, which is what I made in three days of teaching. Never looked back.

**CC:** How long did it take for you to get into a groove with selling and positively impact your financial life?

**AL:** I got connected with somebody locally and started doing parties. But it began slowly. My first few parties were pretty crappy. I worked through that learning curve and figured out the best way to do the business. Within a year, I was earning roughly $1,000 a month extra, above my teaching salary. After three years of working Pure Romance part-time and teaching full-time, my husband and I found out we were expecting our first baby. I was able to make a decision to do the stay-at-home mom thing and leave teaching. That very year, I'd made $70,000 just as a consultant. That's when my business really exploded.

**CC:** What has been the most challenging part of running your own Pure Romance business?

**AL:** The most challenging thing for me is my time balance. I have a husband. I have a ten-year-old. I have a six-year-old. I'm a really hard worker, and sometimes I don't know when to stop. That's not necessarily a bad thing if you love what you do, but it makes it hard to strike the right balance between work and family. I'm home, and work is always here. It's tough for me to close my office door and say, "Okay, I'm done for the day, I don't need to do any more." I'll also drive up to an hour and a half to organize a party.

**CC:** What has been the greatest thing about operating your own business? Is it the independence? The money? The ability to enhance people's intimate relationships? All of the above?

**AL:** For me, honestly, the greatest thing is all of it. In eleven years, it has changed my life. I love being able to work at home and do things on my own time and my own terms. I love the financial independence this job affords me. I love knowing that if I wasn't around, a lot of my customers wouldn't have any other way to buy these products. There is a huge need that I'm able to fill. I also love that I get to sell the luxury brand all others aspire to.

**CC:** What stigma do you personally find is still attached to selling our products? How have you seen it change?

**AL:** I saw much more pushback from people when I started. I'm not sure if that's because people are a little bit more open today to sexual health, or I just have more confidence in what I do and know how to explain it in a better way that is much more descriptive. All I can tell you is, I'm in the middle of farm country, and what I see primarily is interest and curiosity, not taboo. That strikes me as kind of amazing.

**CC:** Can you share your income trajectory from Pure Romance and how it has remained consistent or risen over the years?

**AL:** The sales and income have risen every year for my first thirteen years doing this, and I'm imagining the fourteenth year as well. By April of 2020, I'd already sold $90,000 worth of product for the year, and I got to keep 50 percent of it. That's just from what I sell. Including my bonuses and what the company pays me, I pulled in another $90,000 in personal income in less than four months. That puts me on pace to pretty much duplicate the $260,000 I earned in 2019.

**CC:** How tough was it for you and your team to adjust to the COVID-19 pandemic?

**AL:** I feel a little guilty even saying this, but it wasn't nearly as difficult a transition for me to concentrate my energy on virtual parties. Since 2017, I've focused on a virtual component within my business really hardcore, having noticed a trend of women joining my team who preferred to work from home. So, I took a really deep dive teaching my team how to do it. When we went from in-home to virtual with the pandemic, it was a quick and easy pivot. For my own business, I have a van that's a mobile storefront and carries thousands of dollars in inventory. It works great for the in-home parties. People just come to my van for the after-party and shop. Now, for the virtual parties, I have a fulfillment center inside my office at home.

**CC:** In what ways do you think our company has been changed by the pandemic?

**AL:** We're already seeing in-home parties again. It remains to be seen if they'll consistently be eight people, ten people, fifteen people, or much smaller gatherings for a while. I know, because of the lockdown, we're all craving time together. But the rise of virtual parties on a company-wide basis has changed our game for the long haul. The particular type of pivot we had to make puts another little bit of ammunition into our pocket. It's forced a lot of us to operate outside our comfort zone and grow a new set of sales muscles.

**CC:** Finally, I'm looking for some honest feedback on how you see my leadership.

**AL:** You're a visionary all right. You are always thinking far ahead of everyone. I'll just say that from the time I turned Pure Romance into my full-time gig three years in, you've become a completely different leader. You've grown. You've matured. You're more understanding. You're a better listener. And you truly know your consultant base inside and out. You get to know us as people and have been very open to hearing from us. You've asked me personally for a lot of feedback and trusted me to teach others. Your being so welcoming to new ideas makes all the difference.

# Acknowledgments

There have been so many people who have contributed so much to help me realize my dreams in business and in life.

First, I need to thank my mother, Patty Brisben, for having had the foresight to launch such a promising and ultimately lucrative business as Pure Romance back in the nineties, as well as for bringing me into the mix relatively early on. As a pioneering businesswoman working against the tide, she stayed the course when the road grew rocky time and time again and has always stood out as the very definition of determination and fortitude. On a more personal note, I need to thank Patty for always being hard on me, for never giving up on me, and for pushing me outside my comfort zone. She taught me how to set goals, how to respect money, and how to keep pushing even when I didn't know what the outcome was going to be. She pushed me beyond any limits I thought I had and really helped me uncover my potential. For that and so many other reasons, Mom is everything that this book embodies.

Thank you also to Josh Ephron. I've always said that Patty is the one who founded the company, I'm the driver, and Josh is the moneymaker. Josh drove home the business lesson that you can't eat top-line sales, you can only eat gross profit. This means that too many people worry about how much their company sells rather than how much it makes. Josh also taught me a lot about how to make sure that I was mindful of how to price products, how to architect different sales, and how to design product assortments. He has played an instrumental role in my life and development, personally and professionally.

Greg King changed my life and my future by getting me into Mount Union College. I had to pester him with phone call after phone call after phone call every day to convince him to accept me, since my SAT scores were so low. But Greg never lost faith. He was always in my corner. I don't think I'd be the person I am today if I hadn't gotten that opportunity to attend Mount Union. I came to college a boy and left a man. Greg was instrumental in fostering my evolution, and for that I'm truly grateful.

Wayde Triska was hugely influential in my beginning years in business. He was the first person who taught me how to read a balance sheet, how to understand a profit and loss statement, and how to make sure I was able to go out and negotiate contracts and not simply take the first offer and roll with it. But he also instructed me in how important it was to play our roles, much like my high school and college football coaches had. And he always told me, "Chris, play to your strengths. Let the other people around you do what they do well, and you do what you do well. That will make for a very harmonious company." He was right. I stuck to that axiom from day one, and it's never failed me. Thanks, Wayde.

The day that we hired Suzanne Murray at Pure Romance was an incredibly fortunate one for us. She is so much more than just our Vice President of Multimedia, tirelessly filling roles as collaborator, idea person, spokesperson, and all-around helpmate. She has been indispensable in helping me gather my thoughts to put this book together. She performed countless tasks behind the scenes to make *the secret is YOU* possible. I thank her sincerely.

I also need to give a shout-out to Heather Battles. She is, quite simply, my right hand. She has been there by my side for the past twenty-plus years doing this work with me, weighing in on any product packaging, any ideas that required brainstorming, and anything creative. I so appreciate Heather and all she's done to make my ideas come to life.

Cheryl Force deserves recognition for all the tireless hours she has put in with me on the road and being such an unbelievable partner in helping me communicate in trainings and in speeches and assisting our

# Acknowledgments

consultants as they continue to grow their businesses. I thank her for her diligence and dedication as a valued member of our team.

I also acknowledge Chris Postler for his exceptional guidance and leadership at our corporate office, as well as for all of the energy and enthusiasm he has dedicated to Pure Romance. My appreciation for his stellar contributions is immense.

For two decades, since she was eighteen, Erin Ramey has made me look good. She's been like a family member, diligently working with Patty and coming up with some innovative and amazing products for our company. I send huge thanks her way.

My gratitude also goes out to Ray Richmond, who proved invaluable in helping to craft this book. Not only was he a great team member; he was able to download twenty years of these crazy things in my head and put them together in an organized, clear, concise fashion. In so doing, he permitted me to share my story with the world. I could never have done it on my own.

I send further thanks to my literary agent Claire Gerus, who found the right publisher for this book and has guided us every step of the way.

My appreciation for the members of our Pure Romance Executive Board is boundless. My eternal thanks go out to Andrea Gilbert, Beverly Long, BJ Jones, Cindy Faulkner, Crystal Boles, Heather Dolen, Janna Vukelich, Kelly Anson, Melissa Messenger, Nikki Hughes, Rachael Seeling, Renee Garley, Terri Tassie, and Zara Zay. They have provided me with the one life lesson that I wish I'd have learned early on, which is to talk less and listen more. It's been a blessing to have so many powerful businesswomen in my life who have given me such an assortment of Golden Rule lessons that served to propel me as a professional. I'm forever appreciative of the hard work that all of them have put in and the dedication they demonstrated to their fellow business owners like themselves. Together, we have all succeeded, and together we will have a bright and fruitful future.

And I can't thank our COVID-19 Task Force enough. This talented group of leaders helped us navigate our sales force in 2020 and into 2021 through the pandemic. They were extremely giving of their time and expertise, and their open and honest feedback was invaluable. Thank you to Dana Barish, Cindy Faulkner, Jenni Flickinger, Renee Garley, Andrea Gilbert, Ashley Livermore, Melissa Messenger, Heather Pillow, and Janna Vukelich.

To my wife, Jessica, thank you from the bottom of my heart for always supporting me and all the ideas that I've had in business ventures; for holding down the fort during my days on the road; and for your hours and hours on the phone with me talking through strategy, discussing what I should be thinking of and how to approach situations differently. But more than anything, thank you for being the CEO of our home, loving our children, and being there to support all their events, games, and dance recitals that I couldn't attend. Thank you for being the best mom ever.

Finally, to my three children:

—LC Marie: Thank you for making me a better person, a better dad, and helping me understand that everybody has a path to travel and also needs to follow their heart and their head. I appreciate you showing me the right way to live through your everyday example.

—Max Man: You teach me, and continually remind me, that every day we can get better if we continue to put the work in. I watch how hard you work in academics and in athletics, and I'm super proud to watch your growth and your development.

—Macie Marie: Your strength and your will are something I admire every day, and I'm so excited for what your future is going to bring. You light up every room you walk into with your spirit and energy, and you inspire me to keep growing as a father and as a man.

—To all three: Thank you for the love and care that you give to one another. Always remember that we're a team. And never forget how much your daddy loves you.